I0014580

Virtual Reality Analytics

A Skilltower Institute Dossier

Edited and Published
by Joerg Osarek

With articles by

Carsten Frisch,
Chuck Ian Gordon,
Krzysztof Izdebski,
Petr Legkov,
Maximilian C. Maschmann,
Joerg Osarek,
Alexander Scholz,
Frank Sommerer,
Kevin Williams

Imprint

Virtual Reality Analytics

Copyright © 2016 Joerg Osarek, Skilltower Institute

Order information: http://vr.skilltower.com/

ISBN: 978-3-944218-08-3 eBook Version
ISBN: 978-3-944218-09-0 Print Version

Publisher: Gordon's Arcade™
business unit: Business Publishing
Triftstr. 30, D-61350 Bad Homburg, Germany
CEO: Chuck Ian Gordon
http://business.GordonsArca.de/

Editor: Skilltower Institute™
Joerg Osarek, CEO
Triftstr. 30, D-61350 Bad Homburg, Germany
http://www.skilltower.com/

English Translation of Frank Sommerer's article by Jan Wassermann-Fry
English Proofreading by Oliver Fry

Cover image:
Frog #84027132 © julien tromeur – fotolia.com - extended license tramsformed into VR Frog by Joerg Osarek

Figure 1: Immerse into data: © Andreus, #31970330 – 123rf.com
Figure 9: Stereoscopy Ladies, Public Domain from commons.wikimedia.org
Figure 11: compiled from Presskit of Fairy Lights
Figure 20: VR Treadmill: © rastudio, #52770276 – 123rf.com

photographs of authors provided and © by the authors themselves

All other figures: Own work of Chuck Ian Gordon and Joerg Osarek or downloaded from the great pool of public domain images from pixabay.com

DEDICATION

to all who boldly explore
virtual reality,
mixed reality and
real reality
using chivalry and wisdom.

Figure 1: To boldly dive into Virtual Reality Analytics as deep as no man has dived before

CONTENTS

FOREWORD

Dear Reader,

Virtual Reality (VR) is the big hype right now in 2016. Headsets are hitting the consumer market this year. VR Games, VR showrooms and VR rollercoasters are popping up. Indeed the power of immersion is thrilling. The technology is now far more advanced. Prices are way more affordable than back in the 1990s, where first attempts to introduce VR to the mass market failed.

Now is the time for VR to move from demos to products. It is the time to establish VR business models.

For content creators it is vital to get user data during VR experiences. This is in order to improve those experiences, as people's reactions in VR differ from those using other media. My thinking is that if measurement data on reactions in VR are already being accumulated, there must also be applications for that data in the business intelligence and data warehousing field. I thought maybe it was cranky, maybe I had a bee in my bonnet, as I am always trying to think well ahead of the mainstream. But soon after my Keynote on VR Analytics at the DOAG Conference in November 2015 I was called by Greenlight VR. They were organizing the first "Virtual Reality Analytics Web Summit" in San Francisco, and asked me to moderate a panel. Since then the idea of Virtual Reality Analytics resonates with both individuals and companies around the world. We see an increasing demand for Virtual Reality Analytics. There are companies out there already advanced in their VR Analytics development.

Going much further than traditional Web Shop Analysis technology, VR Analytics promises to deliver far deeper insights into the consumer's psyche which is wonderful on the one hand, but on the other, might be disliked by different parts of the user community. As immersive media are so powerful, it might be a good idea to develop analytical technologies that are based on a consensus of involved parties. And we should do this in a responsible way.

This gains in importance as VR is only the first of three visual computing waves heading our way over the next several years. After VR there will be the AR (Augmented Reality) wave and then the USEMIR wave (Ubiquitous SEnsory MIxed Reality) which will be explained in more detail in this dossier. Each wave will develop its own kind of specialized analytics, enhancing today's BI systems. And the successive waves will transform what we know as Big Data into Gigantic Data (GiganData).

I wish to thank all the co-authors of this dossier for sharing their knowledge with you, so you are on the receiving end of different perspectives on Virtual Reality Analytics.

I hope you enjoy reading the dossier, and maybe one day we meet up in the course of the great adventure that is Virtual Reality Analytics.

Joerg Osarek, May 2016

ABOUT THE AUTHORS
in alphabetical order

Carsten Frisch

With an advanced degree in mathematics Carsten Frisch worked in the Business Intelligence & Data Warehousing area mainly as consultant since 2000. He experienced the first wave of virtual reality in the 1990s with excitement. For many years now Carsten also focuses on Big Data & Analytics - and the digital transformation.

Mail: carstenfrisch154@gmail.com
Profile: https://de.linkedin.com/in/carsten-frisch-b2302ab4

Chuck Ian Gordon

Science fiction author Chuck Ian Gordon has been in the IT game for decades. His debut novel GameW0rldz – a Virtual Reality adventure – , based on current and near-future technological developments and the author's own experiments with AI, throws up important questions for what is to come. Gordon is currently working on the GameW0rldz sequel 3futurez.com – a series of science fiction novels as well as an actual holodeck musical using today's and future VR and AR technology.

Website: http://www.GordonsArca.de/

Krzysztof "RodioR" Izdebski

Hunting ways for "doing more by doing less", Krzysztof studied cognitive science to learn about human effectiveness and how to improve it. Now, using his scientific background, he is doing just that by pursuing VR functional content.

Profile:
https://de.linkedin.com/in/krzysztof-"rodior"-izdebski-62b3a7ba/en

Petr "Razialo" Legkov

Work experience before modern VR taught Petr that to achieve good results that are known to people, you need to develop fast and communicate with public. That is why he specializes in quick prototyping and networking with both developers and end users groups.

Profile:
https://de.linkedin.com/in/petr-legkov-948772117

Maximilian C. Maschmann

Maximilian C. Maschmann is a Virtual Reality enthusiast. Maximilan received his Bachelor's degree in Business Administration with finance as major. After a year as manager for a big fintech startup, he went back to university for his Master's degree in Management with Finance and E-Commerce as major. Since 2014 Maximilian has worked together with his brother on several Virtual Reality projects. In addition to virtual reality analytics, Maximilian is a creator and fan of virtual reality movies. He currently resides in Frankfurt am Main (Germany).

He can be contacted at max@spartan-virtual.com .

Joerg Osarek

If you want to know how your business can profit from Virtual Reality, Joerg Osarek can help you find the answer. Osarek is keynote speaker and IT Management consultant for gamechanging technologies. He is founder of Skilltower Institute that explores subjects always some time ahead of mainstream, strategically, as well as with hands on implementations. Since 2012 Osarek has dived deep into Virtual Reality, specializing in VR analytics and cinematic VR.

His background in 3D computer graphics, dating back to the late 1980s, comes in handy. His personal portfolio ranges from strategy and interim management to hands on architecture and coding of complex IT systems and VR production pipelines. Osarek has worked in IT consulting since 1992 and co-founded the its-people IT consulting business in 2003. He is author of books about consulting and the impact of IT on our civilization.

email: joerg.osarek@skilltower.com .

Alexander Scholz

Alexander Scholz, born in 1974, works as a computer scientist and associate in the its-people group (www.its-people.de). In addition to his main activity as an architectural consultant for databases and virtual systems, he studied journalism at the Free School of Journalism in Berlin. He produces video posts under the brand zukunftsfinger® with the theme "Technology in social responsibility".

He is the first PR-coach for founders and self-employees and orientates the contents of his workshops and seminars on Public Relations and Storymarketing specifically to the needs of the founders. More information about this are available on www.pr4start.de . Privately, he lives with his wife and his two children in Wiesbaden, exercises in Kyudo (japanese archery) and is committed to more political transparency and citizen participation.

Frank Sommerer

Frank Sommerer, IT specialist for CRM since 1993, with a background in Customer Analytics and Business Intelligence, has been working intensively on digital transformation and its influence on cross-channel marketing and CRM. As CEO of a leading software and media company, he built up a direct marketing infrastructure (strategy, architecture, systems, processes, staff) perfectly suited to the company and contributed decisively to its repositioning as a customer-centered target group organization.

As CEO of the ist-peoples Consulting Agency, he developed concepts and strategies to further develop the portfolio. Besides Big Data Analytics, he sees immense business opportunities specifically for Virtual Reality Analytics. He remains convinced that Virtual Reality will soon become the new emotional marketing channel, and shall demonstrate its relevance to business in the very near future.

email: fso@frank-sommerer.de

Kevin Williams

Kevin Williams has an extensive background in the development and sales of the latest amusement and attraction applications and technologies. The UK born specialist in the pay-to-play scene; is well-known and respected through his consultancy KWP; and as a prolific writer and presenter (along with his own news service The Stinger Report), covering the emergence of the new entertainment market.

Kevin has co-authored a book covering the sector called 'The Out-of-Home Interactive Entertainment Frontier' (published by Gower). He is also the founding chairman of the <u>DNA Association</u>, focuses on the digital Out-of-Home interactive entertainment sector. Kevin can be reached at – kwp@thestingerreport.com

THE PRESENT AND THE FUTURE OF VIRTUAL AND AUGMENTED REALITY ANALYTICS

by Joerg Osarek, Skilltower Institute

Abstract

There is huge hype about virtual, augmented and mixed reality (VR/AR/MR). Facebook, Sony, Microsoft, Google, HTC and others are investing billions of dollars. 2016 sees the VR industry entering the mass market for consumers. Immersive media create an impressive reality, surrounding the user completely.

With the analysis of VR/MR experiences, the completely new topic of immersive analytics hits the ground in the just-established big data systems landscape. Who watches which objects for how long? With what facial expressions and what emotions? What mood is which content causing? How to connect this new data stream to your existing data warehouses? What chances and risks arise from that for our business and our society?

A brief personal VR history

Back in 1998 I announced the potential of VR for the internet in a DOAG.org talk. We built some fancy database-generated VRML worlds for some customers. But it was too early for several reasons. Now the relevant technology is advanced and affordable for the mass market to dive into exciting VR experiences. Now is the right time. The hype is underway. The possibility and necessity to analyze user data during VR/MR experiences creates a new branch in the big data analyrics sphere. At the same time immersive media proves to be way more influential than any classic medium before.

The hype started as of Oculus' successful kickstarter campaign - and its acquisition by Facebook for two billion dollars. Since then there is rarely a month without at least one breaking news that has the potential to completely change the game. Be it Microsoft hololens, the 1.4 billion investment in MagicLeap by Google and others, or the showcase of the Lytro Cinema - a lightfield movie camera showing a sample short movie of Maleficent director Robert Stromberg demonstrating how half of the production pipeline for hollywood movies could be disruptively changed.

Name the game: VR, AR, MR=xR

To clarify the names used:

- Virtual Reality (VR) means the complete immersion into another world blocking the real world.

- Augmented Reality (AR) means projecting virtual.information on top of the real world.

- Mixed Reality (MR) means to place artificial information and objects positionally and rotationally correct into 3D space in real time. We shall see which term eventually will be the most commonly used for this. It might be Mixed Reality, Blended Reality or Augmented Reality.

We can sum up the relevant technologies VR/AR/MR as xR.

What is happening at VR/AR/MR?

In Gaming VR is well established already. At the same time a new movement towards cinematic VR has begun, driven by experiments by large studios, like Dreamworks, Disney, Pixar or by cinematic VR specialists like JauntVR. Additional applications are in development, some already succesfully established like VR rollercoasters, VR showrooms, VR scenarios for training, or treatment of phobias.

It is compelling to watch other applications appearing and discover which of them are here to stay.

Examining all those scenarios, one thing is very clear. The analysis of behavioural data during xR experiences is essential. Firstly, to observe user reactions and to improve the experiences. Secondly, to learn about user behaviour in general.

We support Gordon's Arcade in creating science fiction VR movies and in authoring the book "The cinematic VR formula". The broad demand for immersive analytics shows that a bunch of new technologies have to be established to eventually create one or some standardized platforms for VR analytics. Furthermore, it is becoming clear that there is an interest far beyond the currrent VR experience in gathering such analytical information. Gigantic amounts of data will be collected so that Big Data looks like little brother! One could say: VR analytics and AR analytics transform Big Data to insanely Gigantic Data (which I call GiganData). Thus, it is very important to find ways to reduce the amount of data without losing too much information.

The new immersive analytics branch of Big Data:

- analyzes the optimization of xR experiences, thus creating more attractive space which also can be used as higher quality advertising space.

- allows the combination of xR measurement data with additional data, like health-tracking data from smart watches and other devices (pulse, temperature, voice mood analysis, ...)

- creates a new level of comfort for the user and at the same time the risk of a total surveillance (like an omnipresent lie detector)

When I came up with the idea and term, VR analytics, in May 2015, I wasn't sure if it was just an obsession or a crank thing. But only a few months after my VR Analytics Keynote at the DOAG Conference in November 2015 (http://www.slideshare.net/joergosarek/virtual-reality-analytics) I had the honour to moderate a panel at the first Virtual Reality Analytics We Summit (March 2016 in San Francisco), organized by GreenlightVR – a company specialized in Intelligence on the VR market. Many illustrious speakers were attending. From bestseller author Jesse Schell (The art of Game Design) and Jody Medich, Director of Design at the Singularity University, Geoff Skow, founder of FishbowlVR (VR Testing as a Service) to Sunny Webb, Senior R&D Principal at Accenture. There is a separate article in this dossier about the VR Analytics Web Summit.

Now let's delve deeper into the relevant technologies for immersive analytics, a helicopter view and glimpse into the future.

VR is just an old chestnut

There are some historical examples of VR approaches, dating back to the time before color tv. For example - Stanley Grauman Weinbaum's novel : "Pygmalion's Spectacles",1935; the first viewmaster, 1939, which fascinated me later in the 1970s and 1980s with its brilliant stereoscopic images and stories, without any screen door effect by the way; the sensorama from the 1950s; not forgetting the head mounted display of Ivan Sutherland (called The Sword of Damocles), 1968, which provided a primitive augmented reality experience. But then the first major wave of VR appeared in the 1990s. It was a failure because the technology was not very powerful but very expensive. For example Nintendo's VR Boy had a red mono display with a bad resolution and bad latency. But now the second major wave approaches. This time the conditions have changed significantly.

In 2016 VR headsets hit the mass consumer market.

There have been many modern developer kits since the Oculus kickstarter success back in 2012. We were in an experimental phase. In 2014 Google published the blueprints for Google Cardboard, which turns a standard smartphone into a simple VR headset, using just some cardboard, two lenses and a magnetic switch. The amount and quality of content exceeds VR content from the 1990s significantly. 2015 Facebook and Oculus launched their mobile headset created in cooperation with Samsung - the Samsung Gear - for consumers. It also is smartphone based, but offers an increased resolution and additional tracking sensors in the headset. 2016

Samsung announces the Gear 360 - a 2D VR camera. As I am writing this (May 2016) The Oculus Rift and the HTC Vive are available for consumers. The Sony VR Headset for Playstation VR (former project morpheus) is announced for release late 2016.The Microsoft Hololens AR headset is available for developers, who are chosen by Microsoft, for around US dollars 3,000.

Compared to the failure of market entry in the 1990s with high prices and low power, today we have reached a consumer price range with sufficiently advanced technology. It is clear for the industry that this is just the beginning of a technological evolution towards indistinguishable immersion. And it is also very clear: we have taken the first steps on our way.

After initial highly optimistic estimates on speed of market growth, there are now more cautious predictions. At FMX in April 2016 Dr. Jon Peddie, president of Jon Peddie Research, sees a market that will grow, but not overnight. "Virtual reality is a hot topic, but it's not yet a hot market," he said. (http://gfxspeak.com/2016/04/27/a-more-critical-look-at-virtual-reality/) There is a relationship between PC based headsets (Oculus Rift and HTC Vive) and the availability of high end graphics cards that are needed to create excellent VR experiences. Also it is to be expected that wireless headsets will dominate the market in future, because cables disturb the immersion and free movement. Despite these hurdles slowing down market development, the industry is sure about one thing: This is just the beginning of a development that will make VR and AR very important standard interfaces for the interaction between humans and computers.

Indeed VR experiences have an enormous immersive power and cause a strong emotional response, reaching from delight to pure horror. Badly created VR experiences lead to motion sickness (nausea) and can also harm people by injuring them indirectly. If the VR program, for example, suddenly tilts the horizon, the user will instinctively try to keep balance and it is likely that he will fall over. Accordingly creators of VR content have a great responsibility. But they will not be able to avoid all VR accidents, just as the car industry cannot avoid people having accidents in cars.

2014, at the world science fiction convention in London (www.loncon3.org) I showed a VR prototype with a dancing woman from the 3futurez holodeck musical. Even though the camera was static (only rotational tracking) I wasn't able to prevent users from blindly walking into the crowd because the experience was instantly so immersive and so intuitive. They "saw" that there was no crowd in the other world so they figured that they should be able to walk about. To me that was the surprising power of VR - that people intuitively interact with a digital world, using behaviour patterns from the ordinary analogous world. One thing also is for sure. The more people get used to VR experiences, the more the

WOW effect will vanish. This illustrates the importance of increasingly great content for VR.

VR is not just headsets

VR is often equated with head mounted display – or short headsets. But that is not entirely accurate. There are VR fulldomes one can visit in planetariums to beam people into other worlds. Mixed reality sometimes uses tablets or smartphones and sometimes uses a headset as means, like the Microsoft hololens. For the user it seems that it projects objects in realtime onto real space. This way there can be a board game on an empty table, your colleague can sit in an empty chair although he is on another continent. But there are already some very interesting developments that don't need tablets, glasses or headsets.

The first mobile phones or mobile devices with auto stereoscopy are already on the market (like Nintendo 3DS). In shopping malls or at the cinema you can find large autostereoscopic displays. Those are the first steps towards cylinders or domes that can surround us.

Highly interesting are light field displays which allow a correct 3D represantation in space without glasses from any direction. A good example is the light field display of Real-Eyes (www.real-eyes.eu)

There are also some other light field / holographic displays like ZScape Motion displays from Zebra Imaging (http://www.zebraimaging.com/products) or Leia Holographic Reality Displays (https://www.leia3d.com/) . 2014 Google invested over half a billion dollars in Magic Leap who also highly confidentially probably work on some sort of portable light field solution. The funding was increased by several investors in 2015 to about 1.4 billion dollars.

Fairy lights is an interactive plasma hologram floating in the air (http://www.youtube.com/watch?v=AoWi10YVmfE) . Because it works with femtosecond lasers, there is no injury to fingers touching the plasma. The predecessors using nanosecond lasers had this problem.

If we are thinking into the future, here is news that might be of interest. In early 2015 an artificial retina was transplanted to allow a blind person to have their sight restored (article in German: http://www.forschung-und-wissen.de/nachrichten/medizin/kuenstliche-netzhaut-laesst-blinde-wieder-sehen-13372115 and http://www.2-sight.com/argus-ii-rps-pr-en.html). Camera signals are transferred to the eye implant with the help of a portable computer. What is possible with recorded images is also possible with generated images. It is not too hard to imagine that it will be possible in future to directly stimulate nerves with projected images, smells or touch. Mark Zuckerberg recently stated he believes that we soon will be able to send emotions to each others

(http://www.theverge.com/2015/6/30/8873819/mark-zuckerberg-facebook-sending-emotions-soon). Please judge for yourself if you believe this is always a good idea.

Looking at all those examples, it is obvious that a lot has to happen before this technology can be used for room scale immersive installations with prerendered or even interactive content. Yet the direction we are heading in should be apparent now. It is the direction into a world surrounding us with sensory computer technology. I call USEMIR (Ubiquitous SEnsory MIxed Reality). Another article in this dossier describes USEMIR in more detail.

Let us return to the present and the near future looking at alternative projection models for virtual and augmented reality.

Today and in the short term there are several possibilities, ranging from planetariums showing 2D and 3D VR movies (Digital fulldomes) to VR caves (like the Disney DISH – Digital Immersive Showroom http://www.designingdisney.com/content/tour-walt-disney-imagineering-headquarters) which easily could be turned up side down to refit ordinary 3D cinemas to show immersive content with polarized lightweight googles. ILM XLab shows a similar technology using a simple cave setup to enable the user to enter a cinematic quality live projection of a movie world (https://www.youtube.com/watch?v=7T9Dv1aLMbw).

Also collaborative environments like the ones offered by CastAR are quite impressive (http://castar.com/). I had the chance to test an installation in autumn 2015 at the IMMERSED Europe in Spain. A cheap reflective cloth can be placed into a corner with a marker. You wear lightweight polarized glasses with two integrated mini beamers which offer a perfect positional and rotational tracking (6 degrees of freedom). It feels like ordinary 3D glasses you wear at the cinema. I can imagine wearing those for two hours. But I find it hard to imagine wearing a heavy brick like today's headsets for two hours.

To sum this all up, we should not only think about VR headsets, but be open minded about alternative projection methods. The chosen method has a strong influence on possibilities and requirements of Virtual Reality Analytics.

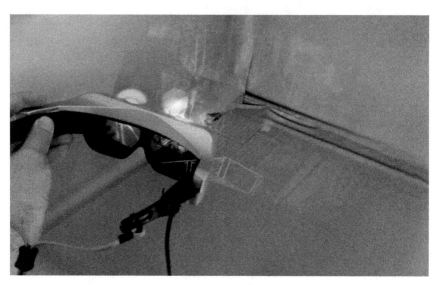

*Figure 2: I tried the CastAR on September 3rd 2015 in Murcia, Spain at the Immersed Europe
Conference of the Immersive Technology Alliance. The image is only visible within a few degrees. Thus
multiple users can collaborate with multiple glasses working on the same 3D scene. Amazing technology.*

Two characteristics of Virtual Reality Analytics

There are two characteristics that the term VR analytics could indicate
and we shouldn't confuse them.

a) visualizing analytical data in VR or AR space. With the transfer of 2D
and 3D display methods into VR space you can gain intuitive insights that
would be hard to explore with traditional visualization techniques. This
characteristic is very fascinating and we can offer customers valuable help
with that. But we are not reviewing this characteristic of VR analytics in this
article.

b) analysis of user experiences in VR space. What can we learn from
behavioural examination of what users experience in VR space? What
insights can be derived from that and how could the VR program possibly
react in real time? Not to forget: How can one build a standardized
analytics platform to integrate it into an (existing) data warehouse? This
second characteristic of VR analytics is what this article is about.

After we made clear that VR and AR are more than just headsets, now
we focus again on the headset to take a closer look at certain technical
perspectives; headsets are the initial mainstream VR channel. Metrics
measured during usage of the headset like head rotation, head movement,
position, angle of view need to be mapped to meaning using a semantic
meta layer. The kind of projection is relevant for this meta layer mapping
process.

A semantic Meta-Layer transforms measurement data to meaning

Option one: pre-rendered VR movies (stereoscopic 360x180 degree videos which can be recorded or computer generated). This kind of projection has some restrictions like only two degrees of freedom (only rotation of the head with tilt and rotation) using a predefined horizon. If the user tilts his head to the side the immersion breaks as the 3D illusion doesn't work anymore. Also the user can't move in the video. The advantage is: It is easier to produce. Youtube has been offering the Youtube VR standard format since 2015 to upload and watch VR videos. With this method of prerendering VR movies we roughly know where the audience is looking.

Option two: 3D scenes completely computed in real time where the user can freely roam around. The user has 6 degrees of freedom (rotational plus positional tracking). We know the exact location of the user in space. Usually game engines are used to accomplish this task. Creating such an experience is more complex and differs from engine to engine. Thus interfaces for VR analytics systems differ too. A small number of companies started offering software to explicitly create VR worlds without the need of programming a single line of code. Their promise: Make it as easy as possible for the user who wants to create a world. Many of those use WebGL, WebVR, ThreeJS. If you chose such a platform make sure you understand if and how to gather behavioural user data to transfer it to your meta layer.

Option three: Hybrid solutions combining pre rendering with more degrees of freedom. One company that offers an impressive possibility to pre render your 3D scenes with 6 degrees of freedom is Nozon with it's VR solution PresenZ (http://www.nozon.com/presenz). They pre render the scene from any possible point in space and retrieve the correct two images at runtime while tracking the users head position and rotation. You can move freely in a 3D image or a 3D animation up to roomscale (15 feet) with your Oculus Rift or HTC Vive. This means that you can walk around in a hollywood quality animated movie. With the advent of light field camera technology from Lytro and Jaunt it is possible to combine both worlds so you also can include real footage within your virtual worlds.

For each of the three options you need to use different techniques to interpret the meaning of user interaction in your meta layer. Only after mapping the measured metrics to the contents of the VR experience can we create information that can be used for business intelligence systems. Such an information, for example, could be: The user followed the red car with his gaze for 12 seconds from second 10 to second 22.

Approaches for displaying VR in headsets

Pre-rendered	Hybrid Rendering	Live 3D in Game Engine
■ YouTube VR or 360°	■ Nozon.com PresenZ	■ (Unity3D, Cryengine, Unreal Engine, ...).
■ VR Player apps, ...	■ some light field tech	

Figure 3: three approaches to VR headset projection that influence the analytics part

Also it might be helpful to include further channels of information like spatial sound. It might be that a user turns his head because he heard a noise behind him.

Mapping today will be mainly manual work, in mid-term automated mappings might be the choice. Google and facebook already use facial recognition and object recognition in images and movies. The automatic transcription of audio in a video is already quite impressive.

If we think about real time generated 3D scenes this turns out to be a bit different. One solution might be to use the rendered images and treat them like the movie in the previous example. A better approach might be to identify the ojects and to determine which objects are in the field of view.

For all options there still is the restriction that the field of view is not equal to the exact location where the user gazed. This could be figured out with a headset with eye tracking like the VR headset Fove (http://www.getfove.com/).

Eventually the task is to record: Who watched which object how long? How fast was his reaction? What can be concluded from that about the user and the experience? What predictions about future user behaviour are possible?

The target of all those data streams may be an existing data warehouse or a new specialized data warehouse that can be accessed to synchronize with other sources of data to acquire a more complete profile of the user.

First companies specialize in VR Analytics

One example is RetinadVR (https://www.retinad.io/). Retinad started with a Unity3D Plugin to collect VR user data. After it was acquired by Rothenberg Ventures the next focus seems to be on creating VR Heatmaps, like we know them from analyzing store shopping or web shopping. In VR Videos and experiences one can measure and discover how attractive is what content for individual users as well as user groups.

Fishbowl VR offers VR Testing as a Service for its customers (https://www.fishbowlvr.com/). If you want to test real world reactions on your app you can just send them your app, define the testers' group and you will receive test videos of the testers with their commentary, a transcription and an anlytical report. This is an important increase in speed for app development as it allows outsourcing of development processes as well as user testing.

Another company focussing on VR Analytics is www.Kosher.tv – a Media Ventures enterprise. Kosher.tv is involved in the US election campaign.

It is just a matter of time until large providers of classical BI systems offer ways to include VR user behavioural data in their BI systems.

The VR Analytics Web Summit (March 2016 in San Francisco) with many well known speakers and industry experts proved that VR analytics already is a significant subject in the USA. Sunny Webb from Accenture leads a 100 person team that create VR experiences including VR Analytics for international customers. This dossier also includes a report about this VR Analytics Web Summit.

Mutual enrichment: Bi-directional integration of open/public data and VR Analytics

Mid to long term probably the major part of the immersive analytics market will be in mixed- and augmented-reality and a smaller part in VR. It is quite logical to place information layer after information layer on top of this world and combine them with MR content.

A wonderful example can be found at the city of Vienna, Austria. A forecast of pollen drift is combined with the local land register of trees, increasing the precision of this local forecast. Only once   complete land registers of trees from Vienna to Frankfurt become available could one use this forecast system to plan a cabriolet tour between both cities.

As the threshold of smartphones having the capacity of permanent internet access and GPS is exceeded, we don't consider it a miracle that we have live traffic information on our maps (Ubiquity). As soon as thecapacity threshold also is also passed for VR/MR and open/public data, new fields of applications will be discovered.

The video that watches back: Emotion Analytics without headsets is reality

Whoever thinks analytical systems only affect those wearing headsets is mistaken.

Like I predicted 2012 at the DOAG conference with my SoMoLo Talk for 2017 the video that watches back already is reality two years early

(http://www.slideshare.net/joergosarek/clipboards/clipboard_somolo).

Development of the relevant technologies is conducted independently from headsets using machine learning and neural networks with an impressive maturity. A great example everybody can test within 5 minutes is the facial expression analysis of affectiva (http://www.affectiva.com) . They use your ordinary web cam while you are watching some test videos and give you a detailed graphical feedback with a diagram that shows your emotional curve during the video compared to the average curve. This way affectiva built the worlds largest emotion database with over 3.2 million analyzed faces from over 75 countries collecting 11 billion emotion data points (numbers from October 2015). The solution is accessible over web as well as offline. Also a SDK is available with which companies can create their own analytical systems. Lately affectiva announced a number of new patent filings regarding emotion based gaming. My affectiva self experiment showed an extraordinary high hit ratio. Obviously I seem to tend to very bold facial expressions compared to the average audience.

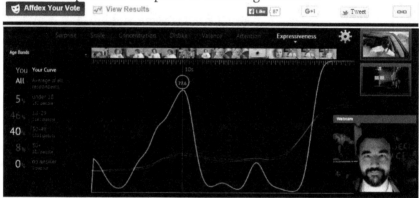

Figure 4: Affectiva: analysis of facial expressions of the audience just using an ordinary webcam (Session of Joerg Osarek from October 2nd 1015)

Mind reading by analyzing eye movement

Using additional technical improvements like eye tracking technology, methods can be automated like the analysis of eye movements as we know it from NLP (neuro linguistic programming).

If you are familiar with NLP, and maybe use it for sales, you know that it is one way to determine what and how a person thinks by analyzing his eye movements. You can find out how he thinks right now. Does he visualize something? Is he remembering or making up something? It is not trivial but achievable to equip analytical SDKs with such functionality. Using the webcam (if the resolution is sufficient) or the eye tracking of your headset this is the next input stream for your VR Analytics data warehouse. Yet it might be a complex task to separate internal dialogue of a person from things he is just watching in VR/AR or in real reality. It sounds a bit like rocket science but taking one step after another it is likely that we will have powerful algorithms to analyse our inner states.

Adding more data sources

After adding rotational and positional tracking, eye tracking and facial expressions, what could be next? A good source of information are smart watches that record body functions. If I watch a VR video, follow a person with my eyes and my heart rate accelerates while the pH value of my skin and my muscle tension changes this might reveal additional insights about my perception of this experience. It might turn out that the physical reactions are quite similar when watching a zombie or a beautiful woman (temperature, heart rate, muscle tension). Probably we would need to have the facial expression included to find out if it is a pleasant or disgusting experience. As fascinating as this all is, we should consider the limits of feeling comfortable with this and of the acceptance within our society about this massively increased amount of data gathering and analysis. Opportunities of helpful usage as well as abuse are huge and already within the focus of the public (some health insurance examples in German: http://www.heise.de/newsticker/meldung/Wearables-Treue-Assistenten-oder-Koerpertrojaner-2835921.html and http://www.heise.de/mac-and-i/meldung/Zuschuss-fuer-die-Apple-Watch-bei-der-Techniker-Krankenkasse-2817046.html)

Transparency is a great good. Maybe it is better to discuss the implications in public while this new analytical medium is in its infancy and agree on rules how to use it than facing investigative discovery by the press provoking a scandal where objectivity has no sufficient weight.

More sources of data may follow like:

- mood analysis from voice information of the VR user

- measurement of environmental data, weather data

- information from other electromagentic spectra like infrared or ultraviolet or other spectra (sharks are able to feel electric fields – why should technical sensors not be able to find hints about us in further spectra?)

Those examples show that techniques like mood analysis, object tracking, eye tracking will accompany us in increasing intensity. We move towards a world where we are surrounded by an "Ubiquitious SEnsory MIxed Reality" – USEMIR. The systems that surround and analyze us permanently will conclude how we react, what we think, what we might do next. Right now we create an infrastructure that is capable of automatically reading our minds. Standardized extensively available public data will help to optimize those systems.

Ubiquitous Sensory Mixed Reality - USEMIR

Those examples of projection technologies, opportunities to measure and analyze our behaviour shows that we need to think further than just VR headsets. They are part of an immersive, responsive IT world with emotional intelligence. We will not only immerse ourselves in it, it is floating around us and will overflow, yes, flood our world. Even if we are not wearing headsets.

In September 2015 I played a little game using brain waves to control it. It was still quite primitive. But if we give technology the adequate time to mature and to be combined with other technology we get to personal insights that George Orwell couldn't even imagine. Meanwhile our AI algorithms improve constantly using increasingly complex neural networks. Step by step the technology surrounding us learns how to read our emotions and our thoughts.

Is this really is what we dream of? Anyway it will happen. With VR analytics, AR analytics and their extended version "USEMIR Analytics" we create a mighty instrument that extends today's big data systems. It enables people, organizations and artificial intelligences to discover our souls as deep as never before.

How to qualify for the 22nd century

Besides the maturity of technology the question arises: how mature are the producers and users of this technology? Two things are worth considering. How we answer them **today** will significantly influence how our future will look like in the 22nd century.

1) How deep do we want to allow anybody/anything to look into our core?
2) What do we want to do to evolve our core?

Eventually this is about the mindset of the human actors in this play.

Status of the Consumer Mindset: 2007 during a TED talk internet pioneer Kevin Kelly announced the end of data privacy within the next couple of years. The current development seems to prove him right. Users and consumers of electronics and information systems should inform themselves about possibilities and reality of the analysis of their behaviour to consciously control their interaction..

Status of the mindset of business intelligence system vendors: Where there is a market for business intelligence (BI) systems they also will be sold or offered based on subscriptions. The trend is fostered by first companies and investors specializing in VR analytics and by focused industry events like the Greenlight VR Analytics Web Summit 2016 (http://www.greenlightvr.com/events/2016-analytics-web-summit). The acting players are increasing their analytical abilities, and thus their power, immensely. As Stan Lee, inventor of Spiderman brilliantly put it: With great power comes great responsibility.

Status of the mindset of BI users in enterprises: Stan Lee's quote also applies to those people who define the details of those systems in their companies to influence their customers in even more subconscious ways. We all face the question: How can we as human culture qualify for the 22nd century surrounded by technology that knows everything about us by taking responsible actions today? As soon as the mind of the machines awakens – and if you research the subject, it is just a question of when, not a question of if – and turns out to be more mighty and more intelligent than us humans, what will it find? How will it judge us? But even if we would stay alone as humans: How do we judge our own thinking and acting? How do we prove worthy to enter the 22nd century?

The simple answer I found after some years of intensive work surprised me at first. The more I think about it the more logical it seems to me.

Our human civilization needs to re learn practicing a culture of chivalry and wisdom. Wise and knightly acting are the key for us to qualify for the 22nd century. There are many more thoughts behind this. But for now it should be enough to sum it up in a simple formula:

$$Q22 = C + W = \text{Chivalry} + \text{Wisdom}$$

Figure 5: The formula to qualify for the 22nd century: Q22=Chivalry + Wisdom

Summary:

The possibilities VR/AR/MR analytics promise over the next years are fascinating. xR analytics and the following USEMIR analytics stand for a new level of personal in-depth-analysis which requires a responsible usage from all involved parties. If we focus on fear and greed, the world will rather move towards dystopia. If we use our possibilities wisely and honourably, wonderful discoveries will enable a better future and a 22nd century worth living in. With each of our daily decisions we lay the foundation for the one or the other path to our future.

SIFTING THROUGH YOUR DATA ON THE HOLODECK! VIRTUAL REALITY ANALYTICS
by Carsten Frisch, Big Data & Analytics Expert

What has become of that wonderful idea of visualising data for analytical purposes in 3D / 4D space - using virtual techniques that allow us to navigate data as if on the Holodeck of Starship Enterprise - sifting through mountains and valleys that signify the highs and lows of data of interest to you - being provided with a near physical sensation of the data's substance - diving through appropriate visualisations for revealing connections in data that are easily overlooked or even totally hidden – managing data for which visualisation in web browsers and the like are not really appropriate, e.g. those big data lakes and their famed aspects of volume, velocity and variety?

Well, one of the most prominent pioneers, SGI, still exists but seems to have refocused on different areas of business. Which are the successors? Are there any?

If you try to find information on this fascinating topic, sooner or later you will find out as much on the web as you could expect (or at least I did), but that it is a bit tricky to get at. How's this? Back in the days when SGI and other pioneers were leading in this sector, that would have been reasonable, because hardware restrictions were very tough and providing such a solution very expensive. By contrast, nowadays all these constraints have softened a lot, or even disappeared. That leads to the question: is there still a need for this and who are the players dealing with it? The answer is: yes, of course there is. And I will show some interesting examples, illustrating very well the power of the VR approach. But first of all let's shed some light on the underlying technologies.

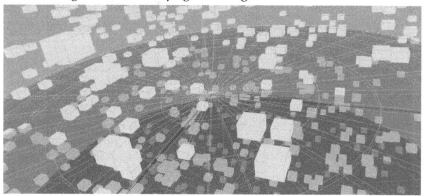

Figure 6: Data exploration in 3D space

Technologies

Virtual Reality Glasses

Virtual reality glasses (one of them - the famous Oculus Rift) typically consist of a pair of 3D goggles or head-mounted displays which are used to show two different images using stereoscopy techniques, whereby the user's brain automatically combines two images into one single image. This leads to a continuous stream of "realistic" visual impressions on the timeline - the projected images provide an illusion of true depth. Computers are used to adjust the images seen by users according to their moves within their virtual environment or "world". This aspect is almost equivalent to that of so called CAVE environments described later in this text.

The aim is to present the user with a "realistic" world which is of course a virtual one but behaves in a similar way to the real world. But one thing still holds: the user is not fully immersed within it. What is needed for this is:

CAVE Virtual Reality

CAVE is an acronym and stands for "CAVE Automatic Virtual Environment". It is this that comes nearest to that what we would call a Holodeck. Such an environment usually takes the form of a cube-like box in which visualizations are displayed by a series of different projectors. It consists of the following:

- Projection walls, ceiling and floor - in typical cases, a six-sided cube or box

- Speakers providing different stereophonic experiences

- Video(s) and sound(s)

- Sensors used for tracking - typically within the constraining walls

The projections which give the illusion of three dimensional stereoscopic images here allow our brain to create the illusion of a "real" space, equal to the first instance. The users' actions are converted in near real-time into a series of images which leads to the basic feature of a CAVE system: Interaction. It is interactions, the immersion into virtual worlds and the combination of both which leads to a phenomenon called "telepresence" in which persons can "loose" themselves within the "virtual world" as if it was real. Users can interact with the virtual objects and / or receive feedback from interactions by using haptic devices such as data gloves and similar sensory mediators. Although systems like these are still early days with regard to haptics and other sensory perceptions, like smell, this really seems to be the beginning of Holodeck technology.

3D/4D VR Modelling Languages: VRML and X3D

Underlying and enabling all the above possibilities of creating a "real", but virtual, reality are, on the computer science side, languages and environments that allow for all this. Virtual Reality Modeling Language (VRML) and its successor Extensible 3D (X3D) are modelling languages going back to the Open Inventor libraries of Silicon Graphics (SGI). They enable modelling in detail of 3D-Scenes in Motion and interactions – which is in fact 4D, when time is considered as a dimension – and had been developed as a human readable standard for the internet. They allow

- for the modelling of animations, sounds, lighting, and other aspects of a virtual world, which are simply called a "world" in this context and their representation in run-time

- for user interaction in run-time

- the use of triggers for external events for example "timers" in run-time

- to add program code such as Java or Scripting link Java Script, JScript,…

Running a "world" in a browser requires a plugin for viewing. The representations of the scenes are generated in real time by the "visitor's" computer. That means that each and every picture will be generated in real time based on the behavior and movements of the "visitor", so complex VR scenes require very high-performance hardware and processor architectures, in particularly fast graphic cards.

Extensible 3D (X3D) is an XML-based enhancement of VRML. It is designed for the same purpose and includes the VRML standard which in X3D is referred to as classic encoding:

- Visualization of 3D animated Virtual Worlds

- Games

- Scientific Visualization

- Interactive and real-time (learning) applications.

Now, what analytics can be done based on these technologies?

Virtual Reality Analytics and Use Cases

One very interesting use case I recently heard of comes from a real world firm that has products for enterprises from the energy sector. They use Oculus Rift virtual reality glasses / head mounted displays in combination with other technologies to create a very special interface and experience for the user.

Let's sketch the scene. In the energy sector as well as in other industries, a failure like a meter outage could be caused for example by a faulty transformer or other malfunction of underlying or connected components. A classic approach to investigate this would be to create a view on a dashboard or on top of a map showing that that failure occurred and where it occurred, eventually also creating an automated alert; once provided with that visualization, you can drill deeper by click down to find the real problem behind the outage.

The solution here is much more sophisticated. A 3D model of that faulty transformer is provided, with signal light(s) signifying that there's something wrong in front of you. A viewer / actor in this VR world could directly interact with the VR model in order to find the root cause for the problem.

The solution is based on an in-memory big data system, and it does not matter where the data actually resides: whether it's in Hadoop or in in-memory columnar stores or relational databases with in-memory options - all those different sources of information are used together to present the data to the user - and I think SQL bridging those worlds and joining all the disparate data sources together actually is, or at least could be, a key element to the solution.

Another interesting use case is Simulation - VR environments often have an integrated event oriented simulation engine, i.e. every object can send or receive an event which can be described by single values or list of values representing time, strings, chars, vectors and ordinary numbers, images or even a whole node of objects and events. What is really interesting here is that the whole system can process this data up to the basic simulation of physical processes!

This is what a Data Center Infrastructure Provider did - they used the VR techniques described above to enable simulation and visualization of the interactions and behavior of the virtual servers and machines inside a data center.

Thinking things further, this might also be used to do some kind of data mining on the data – interpreting and classifying meaning and content and even predict some events (or behavior) in the future which follow necessarily out of the input data. But even the possibility of interacting with the data as if it was a part of the real world can lead to some very interesting and sophisticated analytical applications. And by the way, these VR environments and engines have dealt with what is nowadays called big data even before that buzzword had been born!

So let's try to sketch some analytics that could be done much better with VR than by traditional means:

- Predictive maintenance and operating of industrial facilities like power plants, machines and / or scientific environments like CERN's LHC, GSI's accelerator rings and the like driven by VR Analytics

- Visual VR based Analytics in the context of the development and operating of autonomous driving and other autonomous means of traffic

- VR supported automation of manufacturing processes

- Visualization and analysis of biological and chemical information by VR means

- Visualization and analysis of textual data like Documents, Log Data, Blog Data and the like by VR means

- Simulation and visualization of the interactions going on inside a data center (as currently done as described above)

- Visualizing data used for analytical purposes and build simulations based on this, no matter what the data might look like and from how many different sources it stems, using SQL on Hadoop and SQL Bridges to interconnect it all

- And so on ;-)

Summary

Looking at the possibilities and seeing the applications that already exist, it is only a question of when that we will see a lot of VR driven Analytics in Big Data Ecosystems and that the Data Holodeck will become as ordinary as today's relational databases and dashboards used for analytical purposes. Ok, beam me up Scotty, the future has begun!

P.S.: If you're interested into this and want dig deeper feel free to contact me: carstenfrisch154@gmail.com

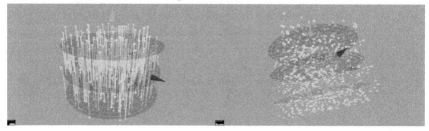

Figure 7: WebGL Data Visualization inspired by the famous Radar of the Elite Game from the 1980s, created by Skilltower Institute

Additional Resources

Extending Carsten Frisch's Article I (Joerg Osarek) compiled some additional developments and resources you might want to follow as in my opinion it represents the technology stack to build web based VR applications on.

- HTML5: (https://en.wikipedia.org/wiki/HTML5) markup language capable of extending the language in itself. Technologies like X3D / X3DOM use that option.

- WebGL: (https://en.wikipedia.org/wiki/WebGL) a JavaScript API for rendering interactive 3D computer graphics and 2D graphics within any compatible web browser without the use of plug-ins.

- Three.js: (https://en.wikipedia.org/wiki/Three.js and http://threejs.org/)

  Three.js is a cross-browser JavaScript library/API used to create and display animated 3D computer graphics in a web browser. Three.js uses WebGL.

- WebVR: (https://mozvr.com/webvr-spec/) WebVR is an (yet) experimental Javascript API that provides access to Virtual Reality devices, such as the Oculus Rift or Google Cardboard, in your browser based on HTML5 and WebGL. Hopefully WebVR might develop into a platform that lets you create VR experiences directly within web pages.

- Game Engines: Major game engines support development of VR content for games and serious applications. Some of them also support running in a WebGL mode to get rid of the need of installing a plugin. The Top league of VR capable game engines include: Unity3D: http://www.unity3d.com ,
  Unreal Engine: https://www.unrealengine.com/ ,
  Cryengine: https://www.cryengine.com/ ,
  Filmengine: http://filmengine.com/ - a spinoff from crytek, focused on cinematic VR content creation and on set previsualization in VR for directors

CHALLENGES OF THE EMERGING VR MARKET: MISTAKES TO AVOID WITH VR/AR ANALYTICS

by Joerg Osarek, Skilltower Institute

In 2016 the VR market is just launching into consumer space. There are challenges on the horizon and there might be mistakes worth avoiding. This article groups some of them.

Big Data is no longer Big Data: The GiganData challenge

Virtual Reality Analytics tranforms Big Data into what I call Insanely GIGantic Data or iGigData, or simply gigantic data (GiganData). Thus far we have been able to collect user behaviour information from smart phone and web site use; VR or AR analytics means the amount of data is at least multiplied and possibly subject to exponential growth. Gaze tracking and positional tracking of the head, body parts (skeleton) together with multiple objects within a VR/AR scene possibly at 90, 120 or more frames per second (fps) result in a huge amount of data. One way to deal with that is interpolation. These techniques are well known from motion capture in the movie and games industries. Motion is captured as single snapshots at e.g. 120 fps. As captured data usually is choppy in some parts, the possibility exists to smooth motion data by simplifying the (bezier) curves, thus reducing the amount of motion points significantly. It is important to reduce the amount of recorded data and at the same time not to lose too much information that would lead to misinterpretations. Nevertheless the amount of data will rise to new heights.

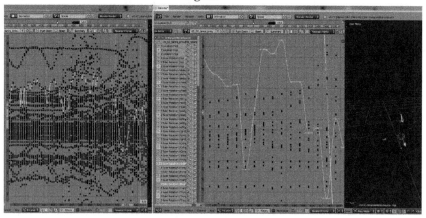

Figure 8: Data reduction – example from Blender – simplify F Curves addon. For a VR Analytics system this has to be done by an automated algorithm.

The technical fragmentation challenge

For now, we face technical fragmentation, due to variety in: a) Headsets b) Display technologies (Game Engine, VR prerendered videos, hybrid render approaches) c) Collection of metric data depending on the technical abilities of a and b d) Data collection process for VR analytics e) VR analytics big data data warehouse architectures. This leads to a fragmentation in the whole chain necessary to build VR content and VR Analytics platforms on top. As Jon Peddie recently published, the industry expects some consolidation for headset manufacturers within the next few years, which will make building standardized VR / AR analytics platforms and information interchange with them easier (http://gfxspeak.com/2016/04/27/a-more-critical-look-at-virtual-reality/).

No matter what the current technology, we all should be aware that there will be a transformation from huge single structure data warehouses to data warehouses with a base structure plus a dynamically defined additional information set per person or/and session. We could call this individualized data warehousing. This will happen because different devices supply different metrics, and a multiplicity of new devices or environments will supply different additional information and formats in the future. Just think of the information cascade from VR headsets, AR headsets, stereoscopic or light field projections and eye tracking without headsets, user motion and user location data with endless interactive experiences and so on.

So on one hand today's technical fragmentation will improve and consolidate. And on the other hand our IT environments, where personal behavioural user data can and will be collected, will diverge in many ways, meaning fragmentation needs to be accepted and integrated into future dynamic business intelligence systems.

The challenge of Standards and content vs. technology improvements

This is another example of the chicken and egg causality dilemma. Producing high quality VR content is an expensive endeavour. Standards are a good tool for easing content creation and allowing broader market access. However, if standards are set too early, they impede the innovation necessary for the production of better content. Let's discuss and work on best practices, but let's avoid early standards that can lock us away from progress for decades – not always to our advantage. For example, the size of the compact disc (CD) was chosen to allow a complete recording of Beethoven's Ninth Symphony on one disc. This led to a CD that unfortunately doesn't fit into the pockets of a shirt. Even today's blue ray discs are the same size. Let's not make the same sort of mistake with VR. We can't predict what long term restrictions and implications might arise from standards set too early in the development stage of VR and AR.

Furthermore, let's not make the boundaries-of-our-imagination-mistake. There was a prediction that there couldn't be more than 3 million cars throughout Europe, because there were only that many coachmen. Kevin Kelly said in his 2007 TED Talk, titled the next 5000 days of the web, "We thought it (the web) was gonna be tv but better. … and it turns out that that's not what it was." The same now. We imagine what a VR / AR / USEMIR (Ubiquitous SEnsory MIxed Reality) world might look like in 5 to 10 years, but we can be pretty sure it will be different. It will change the way we interact with technology and the way technology interacts with us fundamentally. So let us not allow our future to be limited by the limits of our imagination.

Figure 9: Ladies watching stereoscopic images – by Jacob Spoel around 1850 to 1860 – a bit too early for a stereoscopic standard.

The challenge of Data privacy and patents

At a first glance data privacy seems a bit unrelated to patents. But both have an impact on progress and improvement with our VR / AR systems and the related analytics platforms.

Great opportunities to learn and to improve VR experiences lie within the analysis of behavioural data. There are also great opportunities to learn more about people in general and relate that to other information in predicting future actions of people. This could be relevant for marketing, insurance, healthcare and matching to certain jobs. What might be seen as great opportunities by some are seen as dangers by others. There is also a different take on the subject in the US and in Europe. It is a fact that VR / AR analytics will play an important role in future systems. Many companies are working on implementing analytical layers in their products. When I talked to a manager at an important player in the industry about VR analytics, they were already improving their first generation algorithms. Some weeks later I was told they decided to treat their further development confidentially. There may be many good reasons to make such a decision. One might be to protect their investment from idea theft by the competition. Another reason might be not to have a public spotlight on that development. US politicians have already identified VR Analytics as subject to keep an eye on. In April 2016 Senator Franken sent a letter to Oculus CEO, Brendan Iribe, to inquire about how his virtual reality company is utilizing and sharing customers' personal data. (http://techcrunch.com/2016/04/07/sen-franken-wants-to-know-what-oculus-is-doing-with-its-rift-user-data/). With this, VR analytics has already made its debut on the public stage. Hence it might be wise not to secretly collect as much data as possible and wait for scandals to reduce collected and analyzed data. A thoughtful action might be to enter public discussion right now, so there is an upfront political and social consensus. That would also protect the considerable investments currently being made.

Which leads us to patents. Many developments in VR / AR, USEMIR, and also in the related analytics field involve patents. That is not news. Even though VR and VR analytics are hot topics, they do not constitute a hot market, yet some some are already seeing a hidden threat to the whole industry. A manager of a major VR content producer told me, "I fear patent lawsuits could bring the whole market down before it really takes off."

Another look at the fascinating product stack of affectiva is instructive (quote from an affectiva newsletter):

> The U.S. Patent Office granted Affectiva a patent entitled, "Using Affect within a Gaming Context" for software that collects emotional data from a person, including facial expressions and reactions, when they are playing a game. The game logic then changes based on the emotional data that was collected. ...This new patent adds to Affectiva's strategic patent portfolio, totaling seven patents issued and more than 30 pending applications.

This is just one example. If you follow the market closely, especially the mergers and acquisitions and related patents, it is not hard to find material for potential future patent conflicts.

The issues of data privacy and patent protection are candidates for de-railing the emerging VR and VR analytics market just as it is gathering steam. As long as there is a common interest in making the VR industry successful, everything is fine. But more than one speaker at the FMX, May 2016, said: "Now it is the wild west of VR."

When planning budgets for VR and VR analytics projects, it might be prudent to keep a contingency fund for dealing with the issues outlined above.

HOW TO SURF THE NEXT 3 WAVES
OF VISUAL COMPUTING: VR, AR, USEMIR

by Joerg Osarek, Skilltower Institute

Kevin Kelly said in his famous <u>TED Talk 2007 about the web</u>:

"It's amazing – and we are not amazed."

Right now, May 2016, there is huge amazement about virtual reality. As Jon Peddie correctly put it : "VR is a hot topic, but not yet a hot market." (<u>http://gfxspeak.com/2016/04/27/a-more-critical-look-at-virtual-reality/</u>)

But as VR really IS that amazing, it is just a matter of time for it to become a hot market - maybe in another form. Maybe with some troughs of disillusionment, known from Gartner Hype Cycles. But it will be a hot market as people like me have waited their whole lives for it to come true. And now it is happening.

As I have frequently said: VR is not just headsets and we won't all be walking around with bricks strapped to our face. Having investigated things over many years, checking out a lot of different technology and talking to technical and business creatives, I want to share with you what I think will happen within the next few years. These predictions are based on my technological intuition, which has been formed by decades in the IT consulting industry. Of course many things can happen – catastrophies, conflicts, lawsuits, economic downturns, whatever. Anyway I believe this is how it might play out. Here we go.

Figure 10: Waiting to surf the next 3 major waves of visual computing: VR, AR, USEMIR

Three major waves of visual computing

I expect three major waves of visual computing to wash over our shores during the next several years.

Let's make this super simple:

- **Wave 1: The VR wave.** We will put on our VR goggles and are transported to countless virtual dreams - for relaxation as well as for creativity and productivity.

- **Wave 2: The AR wave.** Our goggles are getting smaller and transparent. We will create endless layers of augmented virtual worlds on top of our physical world. We can blend from completely isolated VR to complete transparency, at will.

- **Wave 3: The USEMIR wave.** We will take off our goggles and the magic remains. In urban areas we will be surrounded by an Ubiquitous SEnsory MIxed reality with holographic or light field projection systems. Technology will have grown close to us. It will understand our facial expressions, our body language, our voice and tone. We don't need any computing devices here because we are in their midst. Q-GRINS technologies will play an increasingly important role (Quantum physics/-computing, Genetics/BioTech, Robotics/weak and strong artificial intelligence, Nanotechnology, Space technology).

Now let's take a closer look at the relevant technology behind my thinking. I think it is clear how VR and AR with goggles will evolve. So let us examine technology that supports the third wave: USEMIR. I will just pick a few examples to illustrate my ideas.

- www.affectiva.com: using simple webcams to analyze your facial expressions while you watch a video, holding a growing number of patents on emotion-aware gaming, having built the worlds largest emotion database. I described it in greater detail in another article in this dossier.

- fairy lights: touchable 3D in the air responsive plasma holograms: http://digitalnature.slis.tsukuba.ac.jp/2015/06/fairy-lights-in-femtoseconds/

- leia holographic displays: https://www.leia3d.com/

- real-eyes true light field displays: http://real-eyes.eu/en/ - I examined one myself and talked with the CEOs of RealEyes about the technology and future development possibilities

- creating interactive light fields with user tracking for individual and multiple viewers (see examples below)

- building light field fulldomes – (enhance planetariums) – yes, this means building the holodeck. Even if the numbers of Giga-, Tera-, Petabytes and efforts sound high – technically it is something we can do today. And with some tricks we can do it interactively in real time for a limited amount of people in the audience. This is a favourite platform for running the 3futurez holodeck musical, the making of which I am supporting.

- voice recognition improvements: digital AI assistants with VR/AR avatars will increasingly help with our daily routines – combots (2005-2007 using capital of web.de) was too early and an economic failure, facebook is doing it right now with its chatbots (http://newsroom.fb.com/news/2016/04/messenger-platform-at-f8/) . Many other examples are constantly improving like Apple's Siri, Google's "OK Google" and Microsofts Cortana.

- automatic recognition and interpretation of images and movies, voice (transcription and summing up) and text will be key technologies to automatically process semantics. A speech of mine that was uploaded to youtube was automatically transcribed – and even if the error rate still is too high it is just a matter of time until it is close to human capabilities.

- machine to machine (m2m) communication will increase enormously to negotiate meetings without the need to click, to retrieve information for us but also to do business, gather and use data and to conduct scientific research.

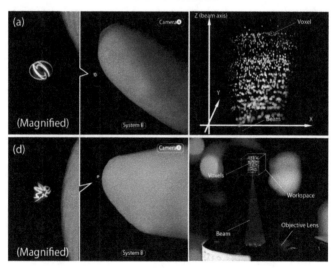

Figure 11: Some examples from the Fairy Lights press kit – a floating reactive plasma hologram

Some thoughts on advertizing in VR / AR / USEMIR

Right now VR and AR are really the best way to collect head tracking and later eye tracking data. But what might arise from that in the near future for the ad industry on the path to USEMIR? Let's think about stereoscopic or light field displays, as mentioned above. It is not too hard to adapt them so that with today's technology they can track a small number of people and provide real time interactive live light field rendering that is responsive to the user. If wanted, individual addressing by analyzing facial features and thus identifying the same person passing by multiple displays is also possible. When you walk through a large station and have such displays on each platform you could continually track a person and provide a continuous story stream - while displaying 2D standard ads for the rest of the people who can't technically be tracked.

In a public space there can be two or three combined light field cameras. The USEMIR systems can scan and rig people and put them into different clothes live or show them a new hat in a light field display. Put them besides a new girlfriend (dating portal ad). But they can also show them things and analyze their reactions. Over multiple uses the systems know our preferences and just show us things that are likely to be of interest to us. Thanks to head and eye tracking only the individual concerned can view his personalized ad and nobody else looking from a different angle. What is on the screens stays a secret between you and the USEMIR systems.

Subtle advertising: Nobody wants to be placed into an ad in VR or AR. We don't want annoying windows to flash into our face while we are slaying the dragon, or indeed when we are crossing a real street. Clever advertisers think about figuring out our preferences and placing interesting objects into our experiences. Why not have a team member wear attractive sun glasses or place cola cans on the table or my favourite drink? Why not let me ride my favourite car in a chase?

How to surf the USEMIR wave

Of course, this is just a glimpse into what is possible with today's technology. The real USEMIR world will probably be way more fantastic, way more dangerous and way more filled with opportunities for business growth and personal development. I can't wait to find out. Now what to do with it? First it is more important than ever to keep your sensors alert for opportunities, and also threats to business, people and organizations. Why also threats? Because every problem can be a gold mine for the one who offers a great solution to the nascent problem. So let's explore, prepare and embrace this future. Let chivalry and wisdom be our guides towards the 22nd century. In the end we all decide what this future world will look like. Or to use the words that are often attributed to Abraham Lincoln: "The best way to predict the future is to invent it."

VR AND JOURNALISM
by Alexander Scholz

In coming years virtual reality applications will develop into a multi-billion dollar market. With regard to journalism virtual reality can generate new formats that define journalism anew, also creating additional revenue opportunities in journalism. VR enables the viewer to be within a scene, rather than just look at a scene from outside. Furthermore, depending on the type of VR experience, a viewer can move freely in the virtual world and view a scene from any viewpoint and any angle. Thus the viewer is within a scene, and can perceive it much more intensely. He feels transported directly to the place. No previous modes of presentation, video, photography or traditional writing, enable the viewer to be in a position to empathize and emotionally engage in a similar way as virtual reality does. This new format is not only applicable to fictional films, but also to journalistic submissions, opening new dimensions to the profession.

Figure 12: VR journalism is a new type of immersive and thus emotion loaded telling of news and facts

First examples available

VR in journalism is not just a theory. There are now the first practical examples of journalistic articles presented in Virtual Reality. In the following some of these application examples are shown.

The most discussed topic at the moment is the refugee crisis. It is therefore not surprising that this issue is also taken up in VR journalism. The issue of refugees is represented in three different VR projects.

In "Project Syria", by Nonny de la Pena, the viewer is positioned within two scenes. The first scene takes place in Aleppo. The viewer sees a busy road intersection when suddenly a rocket strikes and rubble flies randomly. In the second scene the viewer is in the middle of a refugee camp, showing the camp's exponential growth as a result of the huge influx of refugees from Syria.

The VR project, "The Displaced", by The New York Times shows the lives of three refugee children from very different regions. The film describes the life of 11-year-old Oleg from the Ukraine, 12-year-old Hana from Syria and 9-year-old Chuol from South Sudan. These three children are representive of the lives of many refugee children and the project shows their fears andworries, but also hopes.

In "Seeking Home", a project by Associated Press, the viewer is taken to a refugee camp in Calais. In this 360 degree video production, the viewer gains insight into refugee camp life. While refugees are in a permanent state of hope of reaching England, the fact is the camp becomes increasingly their permanent abode.

In addition to VR contributions relating to refugees, there are other issues that have a similar effect on the audience. This includes the Ebola epidemic in Africa. Project "Ebola Outbreak", by Frontline, shows the outbreak and spread of the epidemic on 3D maps. Viewers can either select individual countries and associated scenes, or follow a planned route. From a European perspective the Ebola epidemic was far away and had little impact. Using VR production, it is possible not only to figuratively represent the extent of the epidemic, but do that in a felt manner.

Natural disasters may also be suitable for presentation in VR. For example, the earthquake in Nepal was shown by RYOT in the VR project "The Nepal Quake". The film was made one month after the earthquake, when many charities had already left. It shows the extent of destruction and outstanding re-construction work in the hardest hit areas.

In addition to reporting from crisis areas, there are also VR tours and documentaries. The film "Inside North Korea", by ABCNews, transports the viewer to Pyongyang, the capital of North Korea, providing an insight into a city to which most people cannot travel. In "Discovering Gale Crater", by the Los Angeles Times, the audience can explore regions even further afield. In this guided VR tour the viewer gains insight into the crater surface of Mars, showing that scientific knowledge can be journalistically prepared and displayed in virtual reality.

But also in the field of urban planning journalistic contributions can be enhanced with VR elements. In project "A100 VR" software company Local 17 displayed the construction phase of the A100 motorway in Berlin. The project is using VR elements for the planned motorway route, thus enabling the public to be comprehensively informed long before construction begins. The public can experience the effects of large-scale construction and enter discussion on pros and cons in a more deeply informed way.

But "A100 VR" also shows a completely different VR use potential. VR can be used to display analytical data: a special type of data journalism. Data journalism collects data from various sources and prepares it in a journalistic way so that relations between the various data sources are uncovered and made understandable to the reader. Data analysis in VR journalism goes one step further - a variety of data from different sources is not only collected and analyzed, but made experiential and tangible in a virtual world. An example of such analytical data and viewer experience by way of immersive display is Roller Coaster by the Wall Street Journal. Here up and down movements of the Nasdaq index are represented as a roller coaster ride in a VR movie. Index data is combined with historical events. The viewer therefore knows why there has been an upward or downward movement of the Nasdaq. The presentation of the Nasdaq data as a virtual roller coaster ride leaves the viewer to experience events on the stock market directly. The implementation of analytical data in VR allows a completely new approach to data. Recognizing analytical relationships is easier through VR, because data is presented not only in numbers and graphs, but virtually comes to life in a virtual world.

What challenges need to be resolved?

The examples show that VR has arrived also in journalism. Most productions in VR journalism were completed in 2014/2015. Some, such as the project "A100 VR", are planned for 2016. VR in journalism is still a very new and young form of expression and there is a lot to experiment with and discuss. The examples cited are intended as pilot and lighthouse projects that demonstrate the potential implicit in VR and how this potential can be exploited for journalism. The examples also show the challenges that still need to be resolved before VR in journalism is fit for everyday use and suitable for mass production. Some of these challenges are discussed below.

The most important criteria in journalism are mediumship, relevance and timeliness. Mediumship designates the property that a journalistic contribution has according to the chosen medium. A newspaper report, for example, has a different structure to a video post on the same topic. Mediumship arises in the selection of topics. Although VR is still a very young form of presentation, the audience has expectations for a VR movie. It does not matter whether it is fictional, animated or journalistic. The audience might well expect to be part of the scene and to be able to move freely around in this scene. When planning a journalistic VR contribution this must therefore be considered. With good planning, a large part of the photographic material used can be reused for other forms of presentation. Often journalistic VR movies also incorporate 2D footage in their 3D scenes. The reusability of 2D and 3D material is an important criterion when considering the production cost of VR movies. While the high 3D VR production costs can hardly be reduced, they can be optimized by a pre-planned mutual re-use of VR and ordinary 2D and 3D material. One way is to partly use ordinary video footage in your VR movie. The other way is to incorporate partial 2D renderings of your VR movie in ordinary posts and movies so they can provide additional sources of revenue. When planning a VR contribution, reusability should always be considered.

The second journalistic criterion, relevance, takes into account the interests of viewers or readers using the respective medium and also the subject matter. Not any topic is suitable for any medium. A report on a local dog breed club does not normally appear in the news. With VR productions topic relevance plays a crucial role. The expectation with respect to VR is is that the viewer is fully pulled into the scene. The audience needs visual and acoustic experience of the scene to eventually be part of the scene. This cannot relate to just any topic. The above examples show that what comes across are issues that are of very great public interest, that touch the audience emotionally, that can be discussed controversially and that are sometimes even violent. Unlike conventional video reports, having only good images is insufficient for VR productions. Good VR experiences allow the user to live through situations uncommon in daily routine. And more than just that, they needs to touch him emotionally. These expectations might change with an increasing number of VR productions, but at the moment extraordinary experience when compared to traditional video is key to success. In the selection of topics this must be taken into account. So a successful VR production must pay heed to choosing the topic, but also to correct implementation. I see the selection of topic and implementation in VR as the major challenges in VR journalism. On the one hand the issue must awaken wide, general and emotional interest, on the other the selected scene must not be morally and ethically reprehensible or scare the audience. I will discuss the ethical aspect in more detail below.

The third criterion, timeliness, also has challenges that VR journalsim will have to resolve. Generally speaking, timeliness is always something occurring between two editions. So in a newspaper only today's events are up to date. For a monthly magazine it is always what has happened this month. A VR production has to address timeliness just as any other form of representation. Similar to video documentation timeliness cannot be shoehorned into fixed terms. In principle documentary may be used at any time. The actuality is geared more toward whether the subject is still of interest, or there is a chance of making an issue of public interest. VR productions about refugees are therefore timely, as the issue is currently of great public interest. If the same films had been published two years previously, the success of the films would not have been so great. Although films might have had the same content, public interest was not that high back then and the productions would not have had the same contemporary relevance. Due to the high production costs of VR movies, actuality requires special consideration. Both the pre- and the post-production phase with VR movies are more complex than in normal films. Intensive research, preparation and planning of each scene extends the pre-production phase. Processing of the video footage of VR shoot and postproduction are also extended. This more complex overall production process must be taken into account with regard to timeliness. If the public interest in the topic has already decayed before the movie is released, the film is not up to date and is then seen by fewer viewers. The difficulty here is to know in advance how long public interest will stay high on the subject. Timelineness will be even more important, the more VR journalism is accepted and the more VR movies are produced. Currently, VR journalism is still in an experimental phase. Technical feasibility and implementation are currently more important than actuality. Mediumship and relevance are determining criteria in current development.

Also when it comes to VR movies, ethics and general journalistic working need to be considered. For example a journalistic representation must always be true. In conventional films, everything you see is being filmed. Of course, in large journalistic productions there is a script and a production schedule and maybe some postprocessing of video footage e.g. to blur faces or number plates. Nevertheless, everything that is being filmed is actually taking place. In VR there are two main options. One possibility is that, as with conventional movies, a VR movie is recorderd in 360 by 180 degree in 2D or in 3D. Besides necessary postprocessing and stitching of material it is also "as filmed" but may be manipulated in further ways, like cutting out the camera (Nadar shot), or the cameraman, or parts of props that would disrupt the illusion of being there. The second possibility is that the scene is completely constructed in a game engine. Therefore – if a scene is reconstructed or postprocessed – a VR journalist has a special responsibility. An exact representation of the natural environment might be difficult or impossible. For example, if you want to show the volcanic destruction of ancient Pompeii, you need to reconstruct the scene. Likewise in the case of a more recent event where no (VR) cameras were near, the scenes and actions shown need to be represented as realistically as possible. Although a wide variety of CR scenes are technically possible, the viewer must be able to trust that the scene depicted really exists or existed (closely) in all viewing directions. If parts of the reality are unknown it is important to inform the audience with a text or audio information that the scene is (partly) reconstructed.

As described above for the selection of topics, a VR movie needs to touch the audience emotionally in a special way. When generating emotions in the audience there are major moral and ethical challenges. On one hand there are the emotional expectations of the audience, on the other the film should not frighten people. Especially with films showing war zones or natural disasters, the line between emotional empathy and inhibition can be very fine. Shattered houses grip the viewer emotionally and put him in a receptive mood. But flying body parts might have an inhibitory effect and exceed what is today morally and ethically acceptable in journalism. This has to be considered during the planning of scene or the selection of filmed material. Since the viewer can look around freely in the scene, these moral aspects must be also taken into account in post-production; otherwise spectators when turning might still see ethically violating images.

Apart from the journalistic challenges described above, high production costs are an impediment for VR journalism. Production costs for VR contributions are often way higher than for conventional videos. Already the pre-production costs are higher; and also in the compilation of the researched material and scene planning note has to be taken of VR implementation. This type of planning creates additional work, which is not needed for normal production. Post-production also is more complex. Scenes, often made in a conventional manner, need to be converted, stitched and postprocessed for a VR scene. In addition to the temporal aspect, it involves additional costs for corresponding video editing programs and powerful hardware. In regular reporting the cost of pre-production can be easily calculated and planned. The cost of hardware and software in postproduction are met once and then are amortized in regular productions. VR production technologies (camera, lighting, sound) and costs are different. The VR market is a fast growing and changing market. Uniform standards in VR technology are developing but do not yet exist. It is currently not clear what technology or standards will prevail, or what technical possibilities will exist, for example, in one year. With regular VR productions therefore the camera technology must always be adapted to the current technical possibilities, in order not to lose touch with the fast-evolving VR world. With the advent of light field cameras like the JauntVR neo or the Lytro Immerge completely different approaches seem to arise for constructing real footage directly in 3D space (currently at ultra-high cost). Because professional camera technology is very expensive and up-dated technology is then required, enormous capital and production costs cannot be easily recouped.

The high production costs in the VR journalism are a special challenge. Viewers are willing to pay in only a very limited fashion for journalistic contributions. Refinancing through a ticket method as in classic theater productions is therefore not possible. Also a cross-financing through other journalistic products, such as newspapers or magazines, is inconceivable for regular VR posts. Newspapers or magazines also often suffer from a high cost pressure which leaves little room for expensive VR productions. Financing via advertising revenue is also difficult. Although individual advertising partners can be found, advertisements can be placed only at the beginning or end of the article. A commercial break during a VR contribution would not be acceptable to the audience and currently hinder the desired immersive effect and full experience due in VR. Surreptitious advertising is prohibited and product placements in a journalistic article are currently difficult to imagine, since this reduces the independence of journalism. Therefore new sources of revenue need to be found for regular VR posts in journalism, for this journalistic division to break even or even to be profitable.

Evaluation of VR data can create new revenue

One possible approach for generating sources of revenue could result from VR technology combined with data analysis. In virtual space, the gaze direction of the viewer is known as the currently displayed picture must be determined by the viewing direction. As long as the viewer stays in the virtual space you always know roughly the direction in which the viewer looks and when he changes his viewing angle. This will improve even more with the advent of eye tracking headsets to the mass market which is to be expected over the next few years. A growing number of technical solutions like a combination of Leap motion sensors with VR headsets, or the HTC vive providing roomscale VR are able to record additional motion data of hands or of the body by projecting a virtual skeleton into it. This thus results in an even more complete motion profile of the viewer. From this motion data in a journalistic VR film it can be calculated how long each viewer engaged in what sequence and what is rather uninteresting. The creation and evaluation of this motion profile requires massive data over a period substantially less than a second. Apart from the actual transaction data, the respective image data has to be considered to answer the question, why a viewer has watched something three seconds to the right. This large mass of data and measured values can be evaluated only with a very efficient Big Data application.

Figure 13: Creating additional value with the data collected in immersive journalistic experiences

But what is the benefit of such processed motion analysis? From a journalistic point of view there are three sources of revenue.

Firstly, publishers can **evaluate this data themselves** and publish sequence coverage of the most interesting parts. This sequence coverage should then not necessarily lead to a VR movie. Any other form of presentation is suitable. For example the most interesting content could be taken up in a special issue of a magazine. This special edition can be sold more expensively than the normal magazine. Since the reader's interest is already known before print, it is to be expected that this special edition will sell above average. Also advertisements are easier to find for such a special edition. The relatively easily created special edition thus serves to cross-finance the elaborate VR movie. Nevertheless it has to be taken into account that people act differently in VR and therefore behaviour we take for granted always has to be re-evaluated. We are still in a learning phase.

The second source of income can result from **the sales of data**. The collected data can be sold to advertisers who can draw conclusions from this for future campaigns. So a selection of advertising messages can be made to only deliver content that people are interested in. This results in an increased likelihood of a successful advertising message. If it is a filmed VR experience, the VR movement data can be collected only when the film is finished and seen by the audience. So the advertising message cannot be incorporated into the film, but must be conveyed through other channels in the aftermath. The independence of journalism remains intact, since there is no engagement of the advertisers on the researched material and the presentation of scenes. This funding opportunity can be understood as reverse advertising sales.

The third approach is a possible **sponsorship by large companies and manufacturers of VR technology**. This variation is similar to the second one, only that the sponsorship of the sale of the data is not the main focus, but happens more indirectly. So Facebook, as owner of Oculus Rift, might sponsor VR journalism. Production costs might be paid by Facebook and VR contributions may be nil for viewers. Oculus Rift transmits movement data to Facebook which then is connected to the existing Facebook user profile data. Facebook could use this to optimize their advertising algorhithms. This sponsorship is then compared to a film sponsorship and also does not interfere with the independence of journalism. However, journalistic VR productions would need to apply for certain sponsorings.

Conclusion

As a conclusion it can be said that VR journalism is more than just empty words. There are already the first examples in which journalistic topics are presented and implemented in a virtual environment. In future other examples will follow, and the area of VR journalism will continue to grow. VR journalism will be an addition to the existing media mix, not replace existing forms. For a significant expansion of VR journalism some challenges remain to be solved. Firstly, the selection of topics to be brought into VR have to be in accordance with requirements in terms of relevance, timeliness and mediumship. Secondly, VR movies generate high production costs for which new revenue streams have to be discovered. The analysis of session data in the virtual space can be one of these sources of income, but it will certainly take some time until VR journalism can be produced in a cost-covering way.

VIRTUAL REALITY ANALYTICS - CHANCES AND OPPORTUNITIES FOR BUSINESS SOLUTIONS

by Frank Sommerer, expert on Customer Analytics & Database Marketing, CEO of its-people

Business Intelligence focuses on evaluating large amounts of data. Huge amounts of data are processed and stored as part of a Virtual Reality / Augmented Reality environment. An intelligent evaluation and use of data is not only relevant to the consumer, it also promises enormous opportunities for companies. Virtual Reality / Augmented Reality (VR/AR) is picking up speed and becoming more relevant to business. For Business Intelligence, already more multifaceted and complex through Big Data, this constitutes another push forward.

Virtual Reality Analytics can be defined according to two different criteria.

- On the one hand, as the visual, multidimensional analysis of the plethora of data available through social, local, web and mobile applications. A term often used in this regard is Big Data Visual Analytics. VR headsets enable better and faster identification of connections and dependencies between data in a 3-dimensional space. This constitutes an intuitive analytical environment through which you can delve deeply into datasets, but also actively participate and change data and rules in order to experience simulation possibilities first hand. This opens up entirely new possibilities for simulations of future scenarios. These new analytic possibilities promote a shift towards more investment in predictive systems instead of only focusing on the past and present.

- On the other hand, there is an emphasis on real-time analysis and use of user data during the VR/AR session itself. Recorded data, such as head movements, visual fields, facial expressions, and much more, need to be interpreted and processed correctly in order to represent a coherent virtual world. Especially the field of Augmented Reality will be able to tap into the great potential of these new analytics systems.

Virtual / Augmented Reality 2016

Virtual Reality is one of 2016's hot digital topics. The latest VR headsets are expected to be the next big thing on the market. Virtual Reality was the key theme of the Mobile World Congress 2016 (MWC) in Barcelona. Aided by Samsung's new VR products, Mark Zuckerberg euphorically describes his vision of a Social Augmented Reality Community. Here Samsung and Facebook see a billion-dollar business for many industries and companies, based on the effects of VR/AR. VR/AR enable emotional experiences, creating a wholly new dimension for what was previously seen as the cold and impersonal world of IT and computers. This facilitates customer loyalty through new emotional experiences (see Handelsblatt, published 22 February 2016, www.handelsblatt.de). Thus these realistic and emotional VR experiences are not limited to only opening up new possibilities in the gaming industry.

Companies can draw on a multitude of different approaches to market their products and solutions with more effectiveness and emotion. This may also bring new momentum into training, since training concepts can thereby be better customized to the learner. Enormous opportunities are opened up by having less distractions during VR sessions and through learning concepts that make use of emotion. Today's e-learning concepts have thus far not been able to fulfill the high ambitions placed therein.

Virtual Reality Analytics lays the foundations for VR/AR to be able to fulfill all the user's emotional expectations.

Marketing Virtual / Augmented Reality

Alongside digitization, Virtual Reality was one of the key areas at Europe's largest trade fair for merchandising, the PSI in Düsseldorf (organized by PSI Promotional Product Service Institute, Reed Exhibitions Deutschland GmbH). Here the first VR headsets with internal digital storage devices were introduced as merchandise (such as VR headsets by Just VR for €25 www.justvr.de). Products could be marketed very effectively using VR headsets, a Smartphone and the appropriate apps. For instance, you could test a new car before it were even built or you could stroll around your next holiday destination before even booking the flight. An unbelievably fascinating new world for creative marketers.

Merchandising materials rely on touch and emotion. Using its two core properties, Virtual Reality gives you the feeling of being there in person and thereby opens up a wholly new emotional dimension.

The two core properties of Virtual Reality / Augmented Reality

VR/AR appears to us as real because
- the simulated reality fills up our entire field of vision, which means distractions from other sources are blocked out

- the image in front of your eye realistically shifts according to your head movement (head-tracking)

An intelligent evaluation and use of users' VR/AR experiences is the basis for a highly effective VR/AR solution, independent of whether marketing these products or their experiences. The goal is to optimally experience virtual reality based on analytical insights gathered.

In addition to the VR headsets' providing valuable data (head movement, eye tracking), wearables and health-tracking solutions can also provide important measurement data during the experience. It is important, particularly when creating or testing content with test subjects, to recognize early on whether the actual experiences correspond with expectations.

Questions this might be able to answer:
- What is the user looking at?
- Who is looking where and for how long?
- What mood is triggered by specific events with various user groups?
- Is the user excited, shocked, confused, relaxed, nervous?

In marketing, success is measured against optimal user experience, the ultimate positive experience for the potential buyer. During design and development, the potential users' experiences must be analyzed continually regarding user experience. VR/AR will have to be able to answer the following questions:
- Illustration of use by different users and user groups:
  What contents do they use? How do they interact? What possibilities do they see/recognize and which ones do they not? How do they rate their experiences?

- Monitoring the main features:
  What do the users see and how do they interpret this? How do they interact with the content provided?

- Analysis of behavior:
  VR provides the most emotional experience in the history of computing. How does the user react? What emotions can be measured? How does the user feel?

- The audience, understanding the user:
  Does VR/AR provide users with the desired experience? Does the experience remain the same for differing user groups? Which user group reacts more positively and which more negatively? Does the experience lead to a more positive attitude towards the brand, to a stronger purchasing incentive?

For the last 20 years eye camera technology has been used in direct marketing to determine the effect of advertising, leading to many optimizations. The applied sciences provide us with great insights into how people perceive advertising and what its effects are. Designing merchandise with attention to psychological perspectives improved quality and success. Over the last 10 years, new findings in brain research (in particular concerning the brain's limbic system) have led to many great insights into the effectiveness of advertising and the purchase-decision-making process. Neuro-marketing describes the insights gathered through neurological research into advertising and brand leadership. Virtual Reality / Augmented Reality possess great potential to better identify and tap into the specific emotional and motivational world of the customer's brain.

One of the key outcomes of this research is the development of a map of emotions based on the three emotional systems of stimulation, dominance and balance, which basically describe us as people. Dr. Hans Georg Häusl illustrates this to us clearly using his limbic map®. Our individual experiences and values usually comprise two emotional systems:

- Adventure/thrill is a mixture of dominance and stimulation

- Fantasy/pleasure is a mixture of balance and stimulation

- Discipline/control is a mixture of balance and dominance

Age and gender have a large effect on our motivational and emotional systems due to the different circulating neurotransmitters within the brain. These do not remain constant over time and adapt depending on age and living situation.

Successful brands possess a stable position in terms of emotion and values represented to the customer, and are thereby already much more successful than their competitors. They unconsciously, or sometimes consciously, guide us to become loyal customers. In this way we might unconsciously grab a specific item as the product triggers positive associations in our brain; all of which we are often unaware of. Our brain is continually performing decision-making processes and has learned to perform almost all of them automatically and without our knowledge.

New opportunities arise through the combination of these neuro-marketing insights with VR/AR experience measurement, which opens up new avenues for the evaluation of marketing effects and Customer Experience. Insights include:

- The effect of users' customized customer journeys

- The perception of brand promise and marketing messages

- The mid-term effect of VR/AR experiences on consumer behavior

- Story-telling, how marketing stories are processed in the brain and how these stories are perceived

VR/AR enables the next generation of storytelling, with the customer no longer looking on but standing right in the middle. There is a demand for producers and film makers to help companies looking to advertise attain more success. In future gaming developers with backgrounds in storytelling will be asked to implement these adverts, rather than traditional web developers.

Example: car manufacturers

Leading the way in the use of new media and marketing techniques are car manufacturers, since the decision of whether or not to buy a brand or model is often an emotional one. Thus BMW now offers virtual test drives with the new i8 and i3 models. Here you first configure your ideal vehicle using an app, then perform a virtual test drive. An exciting experience... Links:

http://www.effekt-etage.de/homepage/_awards/BMW_Samsung_VR_App.html
https://www.youtube.com/watch?v=MlNaog8Aw3s

Figure 14: Various car manufacturers started their first VR showrooms with surprising results

Example: Augmented Reality app by Villeroy & Boch - A new bathroom planning experience

This app lets the customer move around his virtual bathroom and place products in it in order to get a good idea at the planning stage of what it will look like in future, how a new bath will look with different degrees of sunlight, or in the evening, with or without lights. Links:
http://www.villeroy-boch.com/our-products/bath-and-wellness/bathroom-design/planning-tools/augmented-reality-app.html

Virtual Reality / Augmented Reality for training purposes

In the field of training, Virtual Reality allows for many innovative learning approaches to e-learning. These possibilities are more realistic and complex than the simulations available today. With the aid of Virtual Reality Sessions, new skills and technologies can be acquired within a safe environment. How to behave in emergencies can also be practiced much more realistically. The virtual environment allows you to move around freely in a three-dimensional space, interact accordingly and experience the consequences of your own decisions first-hand. The main advantage: Nothing breaks if you fail ("the freedom to fail"). Critical skills can be acquired in the most diverse of industries without risks, more effectively and at less cost than today.

The inclusion of gamification enables learners to identify problem-solving techniques, develop them further and test them in various different applications. Being able to concentrate fully on a task and the more emotional VR/AR environment means learners are more motivated and more committed to learning. This produces significantly better learning experiences, which are also more likely to have a positive effect on long-term memory.

According to one manufacturer: Virtual Reality is the best thing to happen to learning technology since the internet!

I recommend LearnBrite's white paper
http://learnbrite.com/learnbrite-platform-white-paper/
and some examples from e-learning studios
http://www.e-learningstudios.com regarding this topic.

Virtual Reality Analytics - the challenge of positive experiences

One big challenge is well-coordinated synchronization, so that movements processed in the brain conform with the images seen. Otherwise cyber sickness can quickly turn a pleasant experience to a disaster. This effect can be reduced using special VR Analytics algorithms.

The brain can only absorb information by focusing on a specific point in the field of vision. This partially occurs consciously, but there is also an unconscious component. Following perception, the brain performs an assessment and compares the data with previously stored information. Whilst performing the assessment, correlations are formed, connections made and emotions triggered. If a strong enough emotion is triggered, the reaction can be measured, for instance using pupil dilation or a change in skin resistance. Outside of the focal point, only around 1/4 of information is perceived, in particular movements and objects that activate our primary instincts and trigger an appropriate reaction or distraction. With those VR goggle test subjects who are also given measuring instruments, it is recommended that after the VR session they be interviewed still wearing the VR headsets, to compare perceived experiences with results actually measured. This ensures measured and perceived emotions are interpreted accurately. Initial approaches in measuring emotions, immersive experiences and facial movements by VR users have shown promise (e.g. Retinad, CognitiveVR).

Since Fall 2015, Germany's largest amusement park (Europapark Rust) boasts the first rollercoaster with VR headsets, where an adventure story is told by coordinating it with the bends and positions along the rollercoaster ride. Here the story is aligned with the positions along the ride several times per second in order to ensure the two remain synchronized, making adjustments where necessary.

http://www.europapark.de/en/park/attractions-shows/alpenexpress-coastiality

Figure 15: VR rollercoasters are the latest trend to add value and fun and to protect mature investments

Analysis requirements for VR applications now not only come from the marketing side, but increasingly stem from creative departments and VR application producers. They themselves define how they wish to use the medium and what effect the story should produce. This can guide people to switch their attention to a particular object as opposed to hoping to catch their attention. This enables deliberate guiding of a user with the risk of manipulation.

Future vision – self-optimizing software

Perfectly working Office applications such as Word and PowerPoint, which can optimize themselves based on usage with VR headsets! Intelligent analytics identify how specific features are used by particular groups of users, and self-learning algorithms customize the interface specifically to the user's method of working. Features that are used frequently are represented more distinctively, and features not needed at the moment would disappear. With features where a user appeared to be struggling, a corresponding "Help" option would open up according to the respective learning behavior. Virtual Reality Analytics would be able to accurately identify and interpret such behavior. The end result would be an Office environment (Word, Excel, Powerpoint) that was perfectly tailored to the user, greatly increasing productivity. Such a customizable product would be very valuable and would establish a very high level of customer loyalty to the manufacturer. This is why Facebook and Samsung see VR/AR as the Holy Grail in terms of customer retention and corresponding earnings potential.

Is this Science Fiction? No, I am certain there will soon be solutions in this field that shall increase our productivity significantly. In my mind's eye, I see many of my colleagues spending hours trying to optimize their PowerPoint presentations in despair, since their formatting alterations do not have the desired effect and lead to other unforeseen formatting effects, for instance when attempting to import slides from other presentations. I see a huge room for improvement in productivity with the daily use of these popular Office tools.

Virtual Reality / Augmented Reality will continue to drastically change our future. I expect a similar effect to that of mobile/social usage with the advent of the iPhone and iPad... both for consumers and businesses alike!

USING VR ANALYTICS TO INCREASE
CONVERSION RATES OF ADVERTISING
by Maximilian C. Maschmann

When it comes to successful push online marketing, there a two key factors.

The first one is traffic. You need people to see your products or offered services.

The second one is the conversion. The online advertising must convert some of the traffic into sales. The conversion rate is defined as the percentage of visitors who take a desired action. In most cases the desired action is a sale.

Good push online advertising will always include both factors. They are linked together as a strong unit.

On the one hand, you can have an immense traffic, but when your conversion rate is near zero, you are burning money. Nobody buys your product or there is no demand for your business service.

On the other hand, without good traffic a perfect conversion rate won't lead to a lot of sales. So you need both, a lot of traffic and a good conversion rate, for a successful marketing campaign.

In this Chapter of the book we are taking a look how VR Analytics can help you to get a better conversion rate, the influence of traffic isn't part of this chapter.

Figure 16: Traffic and Conversion need to be balanced in modern commercial IT systems

A lot of the classic advertisers have a big problem.

They don't have a lot of data about their customers. So they are wasting a lot of their marketing budget. Or maybe they have data, but they don't use it the right way.

Henry Ford once said, he knew half of every dollar he spent on advertising was wasted. He just didn't know which half.

When it comes to advertising in virtual reality, then VR Analytics is the key factor to success.

Wouldn't it be nice if you had unlimited data about your customer, so you wouldn't waste your budget anymore?

This chapter is about optimizing the conversion rate in VR. We will take a look at three different perspectives. The first one will be about building narrow target groups and how to reach them without drop losses. This one is also about setting the right rules and filters for the algorithm. The second one is about how you can use eye tracking to achieve a higher conversion rate. The last one is about the perfect pricing in VR stores for a better conversion rate.

First perspective

The first perspective is a close look at the use of secondary personal data. An ideal case would be to use the connections of the virtual reality stores like the Oculus store and social networks like Facebook. This personal data is very suitable for building narrow target groups for each of your campaigns. You can use the information on preferences, likes, relationship status, sexual orientation and so on from the social network.

Then you combine this information with the specifications from the virtual reality store or platform like age, sex, height, location, played games, watched movies and so on. The result is a big mix of data about your customer.

The next step is how we can use this big mix of data about our customers to increase our conversion rates. For this step we have to build very narrow target groups first.

For this we need two things, good market research and good product managers who know their products and customers. For the last step we use this information on what our narrow target groups look like and set our rules and filters for the algorithm when our advertising will be shown. You can compare this to Facebook marketing, which also sounds complicated but in reality is very easy to operate. The following case study is to show you how simple this is.

Case Study example US based Baseball Cap Company

For this example, we take a company for baseball caps.

To make it easy, the company has only one single product, baseball caps.

They have an online shop and you can buy them in several offline sport retail stores.

They only sell and ship them in the USA, not in any other country.

The company has done market research and knows that 98% of their customers are males. And their key customers are age 14 to 30.

The sexual orientation of their costumers is 99% straight.

The last thing they know is, that almost all of their customers are big baseball fans.

The marketing department is very interested in an advertising campaign in a VR videogame. They split the budget in half and give it to two Virtual Reality advertising agencies. The first agency (agency A) isn't very clever, they don't build any target groups and set any filters at all. So the advertising for the baseball cap company will be in any VR videogame. They also don't use any filter for the geolocation.

The japanese 60 years old man who plays a quiz game will see it the same way as the 14-year-old canadian girl playing a strategy girls game.

The other agency (agency B) is clever, they use VR analytics. First they build a very narrow target group and set the following rules and filters for the algorithm.

-Only males

-Only in age between 14 to 30

- Only straight sexual orientation

- Geolocation only in the USA

- Then the rule that the person must satisfy one of the following terms:

Should have liked a Baseball fan page or player or club in Facebook

Had played or installed a baseball Game in VR

Had recently watched VR Videos about Baseball.

Then the algorithm only shows the advertising to users who fit these rules and filters.

I don't have to mention which agency has a better conversion rate.

This case study shows you how VR Analytics of secondary user data is perfect to boost the conversation rate.

There are a lot more advantages to VR Analytics with secondary data.

With VR Analytics advertising for long tail products could also be much easier. Advertising for long tail products via television or other channels was not very economical in the past. But with VR Analytics it could lead to very good conversion rates in the future. Think of small-sized enterprises, like retailers or restaurants. Advertising could reach only people who have the geolocation actually based in their area and fit within their target groups. Or wedding products could only be shown to people who had their engagement recently (this data is already easily obtainable from Facebook).

Another great advantage is personalized advertising for the same product but for different target groups. For example, when it comes to cars, women pay more need to a good looking interior and a good design. Men pay more need to power and technical highlights. Families with young children pay more need to safety. Younger women are looking for fancy colors. Some other people are looking more for environmental sustainability and social responsibility. With the secondary data you have from Facebook and the extended one from your store you could instead of only showing one advertising for all of them, show different advertising for each target group. This strategy will optimize your conversion rates.

The last technique for the perspective shown in this chapter is re-targeting. With the data from, for example, the users' internet browser, you can make crossmedia re-targeting to the same user in the virtual reality. If someone was browsing for Levis jeans in his browser, you can retarget him in the VR. You are showing him advertising for Levis. This tool or technique, often used in online marketing, will help you to boost your conversion rates.

Concluding this perspective, its critics should be mentioned.
When the Oculus store first came out, there was a lot of criticism about the data it collects about users. The data collecting debate will go on: what is of major advantage for advertising agencies and companies may be a disadvantage for users.

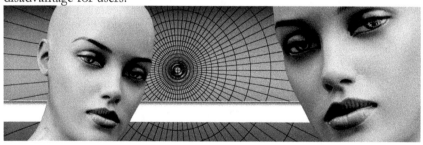

Figure 17: Different viewpoints on collected data from VR experiences are likely

Second perspective

The next important perspective is eye tracking.

Eye tracking is known as the process of measuring either the point of gaze (where one is looking) or the motion of an eye relative to the head.

Eye Tracking is the next big step to make for VR and VR Analytics.

But using eye tracking for a better conversion of advertising is nothing new. Devices for eye tracking have been used for years to optimize real life stores, print advertising and video ads. There are plenty of data analytics tools for eye tracking. This chapter was written before eye tracking was a mass market specification in head mounted displays. SMI, a german company specialized in eye tracking devices for marketing, has developed an upgrade system to implant eye tracking into the Developer Kid 2 from the Oculus Rift.

And the Fove, a new head mounted display coming out 2016, will be the first mass market public head mounted display to include eye tracking.

In November 2015, at the VRX Conference in San Francisco, Jesse Schell, the CEO of Schell Games, shared his thoughts on where the VR industry is heading over the next 10 years. His prediction is that by 2020, VR headsets including eye tracking will be available.

Eye tracking will help you to optimize where advertising, for example in games, will best be shown. You can analyze where each specific user is looking when he plays a game, or when he is doing other things in the VR. With that optimization you can show the advertising exactly where people are looking. You are not losing the "traffic" of people to whom the advertising is addressed without their noticing.

But here there are some critical voices against advertising in VR experiences. The critics say that advertising in VR could destroy the immersion/presence of the user. When a user is watching a very immersive VR movie and you interrupt it with an advertising break or banner/display advertising, you are destroying his great experience.

This is not very user friendly. But these ideas are also very important for every advertising agency. If you destroy the great experience, this will have a negative influence and could furthermore be negative for the product brand.

One of the solutions could be a product placement in the movies or videogames. This won't destroy the VR experience. And here eye tracking could be the important factor. Because in regular movies there is the problem of product placement not being noticed. In VR movies this problem would be even bigger, because here you have a 360 degree surrounding, and the chance of missing the product is even bigger.

But with eye tracking and VR Analytics you have a solution to this problem. You can analyze where the users are looking in the videogame or movie. Then you can optimize the product placement so that the user's eyes will encounter it.

For better understanding, we have a little example.

We take a driving sequence from a VR movie. The avatar (user) sits in the front of the car. You have a product placement in the form of a shopping bag from a famous brand in the backseat. But only a few users turn their heads in this sequence and actually see the shopping bag and the brand. The company is loosing money. The conversion rate will be very low.By analyzing eye tracking data, you find out that in this sequence most people glance several times at the car's radio and navigation system.

As a conclusion, you could place a product, for example, a coffee cup from a famous coffee company next to it.

This product placement would have a better conversion.

Maybe this sounds very complicated, but it is not a problem with good VR Analytics. You can collect eye tracking data from everything the users are doing in the VR. With good analytics you can optimize future product placements based on this data.

Another way could be market research before making the movie. You could simply build the movie sequences in a system-like unity and show it to a sample group. Then with the eye tracking data from this sample group, you can optimize product placement in the final scenes of the movie. You can compare this approach to predictive behavioral targeting in online marketing.

Third perspective

The last part of this chapter focuses on how VR stores, like the Oculus Store, can achieve a better conversion rate with VR Analytics by adopting individual pricing.

First of all, most people know that, with the right data about their customers, it's easy for stores to present the right titles for each customer. This is simply based on the data analyzed of recent buying of games and movies. This simple technique will optimize your conversion rates. Almost every online shop is doing this right now. Together with analytics of personal data from social networks, like Facebook, and browser data, we can optimize this even more.

But besides that basic knowledge there is a more advanced possibility of achieving better conversion rates and make extra profits.

We are talking here about price discrimination. In VR stores it could work perfectly, because all products in VR Stores are digital goods. A digital good exists only in <u>digital</u> form. It has strongly decreasing average unit costs (first copy costs). The following copy costs for a VR Media product are near zero.

This allows the store an easy to use first degree price discrimination. This requires the store to be a monopoly seller of the digital good. But this is easier than it sounds. With an exclusive title, like a movie or a videogame only for your store, you can easily be the monopolist for a product. With VR Analytics you will be able to know the absolute maximum price (or <u>reservation price</u>) that every user is willing to pay. By knowing this you are able to sell your digital good to each user at the maximum price he is willing to pay. In this case we have no <u>deadweight loss</u> and very good conversion rates. But there is criticism about this individual price for everyone and there are considerations in some countries about banning this.

For a better understanding of this perspective, just see the following case study.

Case study

Scenario 1:

The VR store, "Fantasy VR Store ", has an exclusive video game. So the store is the monopolist for this title. It has a price of 9,99$. At this moment there are three store users interested in the product. For user A, it`s a cheap price, he likes the game, so he buys it. Conversely, for user B, who also likes the game, the price is too high. So he doesn't buy it. User C sees the game, but does not like the graphics of it. He doesn't buy it. At this moment the store has a conversion of 33,33% and overall sales of 9,99$.

Scenario 2:

The same VR store as in scenario 1 and the same exclusive product.

But this time the VR store manager is clever and uses VR Analytics to analyze the users' data. The store makes a first degree price discrimination for every customer.

We have the same users from scenario 1. This time user A gets the price 12,50$, because this is the maximum price he is willing to pay according to the analytics. User A buys the video game for 12,50$. For user B the maximum price is 7,50$, so the store offers him the game for 7,50$. User B buys the game.

As in scenario 1, user C doesn't like the graphics, so he doesn`t buy the game.

The conclusion is the store had a 66,66% percent conversion rate, better than in scenario 1. As a bonus, overall sales also were much better, in this case the store made 20,00$.

THE HEART OF VR: FUNCTIONAL CONTENT
by Krzysztof Izdebski and Petr Legkov

Half a year ago my brother asked me, "Why should I buy VR goggles?". With my usual excitment, I was explaining to him how VR is a new medium, how much more engaging games are, how much more immersive the storytelling is. After a few minutes he stopped me, and just asked, "Yeah, that's cool. But why do I NEED it?" Ever since I have been researching exactly this question: why would anyone buy a virtual reality setup?

What are the content types out there?

Right now, the biggest marketing efforts are aimed at gamers. There are many good reasons for that, such as the fact that many gamers already have graphic cards powerful enough to run VR smoothly, or that "being there", in the game world itself, is the dream of most gamers.

Now, games are all right, and they provide a lot of fun, but is that all that we can do with VR? While the vast majority of current development methods are put into games, there are many other types of VR content that differ from games by more than just use case.

First off, lets look at what types of content there are. A first, rough distinction can be made between that content created for entertainment and that for serious uses. Entertainment content is almost always aimed at the mass market with as wide and versatile a target group as possible. Meanwhile, serious content aims usually at a specific target group or specific use context. Now, being categorized as serious content does not automatically make content functional, but we will come back to that in just a moment.

Entertainment

Both of these rough distinctions vary in themselves - and there are categories. In entertainment, we can differentiate fourcategories:

- games – following a long history, game applications have goals, scoring, competition or cooperation, as well as many other features that are well described in game theory;

- experiences – while very similar to games from an artistic point of view – both are based on animations and 3D real time rendering – the design rules and framework differ: experiences do not need goal, scoring, etc., but rather focus on experiential values, such as storytelling or relaxation;

- 360 video – even though technology to record in 360 degrees was available before, only thanks to modern HMD technology has this type of content gained hugely in popularity; now we see a lot of content from private users to professionals; this 360 video is a new medium that is still widely unexplored;

- social – probably the most promising and powerful type of entertainment content, where people can meet in a virtual environment, having a vivid sense of "being there", even if they are hundreds of miles away, become whoever they want to be, and, most of all, still interact with other people by means ranging from simple interactions like button press (e.g. gamepad), through hand movements (e.g. Leap Motion), to the whole body tracking (e.g. Kinect).

All in all, entertainment apps are about the experience itself – the experiential value, the pleasure, the memorability.

Serious

Similarly to entertainment, in serious content we can differentiate five categories:

- education – using VR, educational methods can evolve into much more interactive and engaging approaches, such as enabling, but not limited to, instant travel through space (e.g. to see the pyramids or the ruins of Forum Romanum), and through time (e.g. Forum Romanum during rush hours in ancient times);

- marketing – in contrast to all the other types of content, there is no agreement as to categorization in marketing, since it is not obviously serious content-wise as others; in a sense it is close to entertainment, since those apps should be a memorable experience; however, since the goal of creating marketing content is not just experiential value for user, but actually informing or convincing, it is treated here as serious content;

- medical – considering the worldwide healthcare's economic problems, it is important to develop new, cheap, and easily available therapies and rehabilitations methods; this is the second, after games, most spoken of use case of modern VR;

- sales – using modern VR, new possibilities for retail, online shopping, product customization and more are enabled –

customers can try out clothes, see a house before it's built, or choose colors of a car interior while virtually setting inside;

- industrial – this is the only type of content that was already extensively explored using old virtual reality technologies, such as CAVEs, powerwalls or "Pre-Oculus" HMDs; while there are already a lot of use cases explored, industrial content was not widely distributed due to visual quality, costs, and many other limitations; the examples here are apps used for design validation, virtual prototyping or ergonomics.

Serious content is created with a specific goal – educational app would be created to support learning process, marketing to increase public knowledgeability of product or concept, medical to treat a specific dysfunction, sales to improve customers' experience and industrial to respond to decrease costs of production.

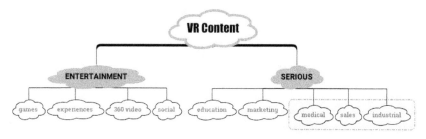

Figure 18: Virtual reality content categorization

What is the focus of content?

"Form follows content", as an old User Experience design saying, which, without exception, applies to VR content too. There are many approaches to categories: describe and plan an application, consider target group, business model, internal or external project motivations, and many more.

However, just as in project planning, we can simplify VR application to three focus points: engagement, high fidelity and functionality. And just as the trade-off between time, costs and resources plays the key role in project management, the trade-off between those three is playing a major role in VR content creation.

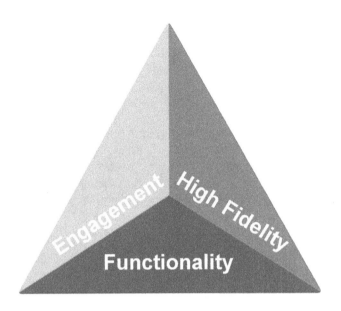

Figure 19: : Trade-off between focus points of content creation

Engagement

Engagement, sometimes also referred to as "The Flow", describes the involvement of a user in the content. From the perspective of virtual reality, some of the most important factors encompassing an experience of the flow are:

- strong concentration on the present moment – similarly to desktop computer games, movies, and other entertainment content, the goal is to forget about anything else, and focus just on a given application; considering that by putting an HMD on, the visual input of real world is shut off, VR strongly facilitates this feature;

- A sense of personal control or agency over the situation or activity – this feature is particularly interesting for VR, thanks to all the peripheral devices that work extremely intuitively when combined with HMD - unlike anytime before modern VR, now we can shut off the real world by putting on VR goggles and still interact in the virtual world using our own hands, fingers, head or even body position.

Following Jeanne Nakamura and Csíkszentmihályi, four other features of the flow are: merging of action and awareness, a loss of reflective self-consciousness, a distortion of temporal experience (know as time dilation), one's subjective experience of time is altered, experience of the activity as intrinsically rewarding, also referred to as autotelic experience.

The Flow strongly corresponds to the quality of an experience – basically the better the feeling of flow, the more entertained the user is. That is why entertainment content, especially games, have engagement as the main focus.

High Fidelity

Fidelity describes how close to the real world stimulus or situation, a simulation, or illusion is. In the context of virtual reality, high fidelity usually refers to high quality or realistic graphics. However, visual information is not the only feature to consider. Many VR developers have already realized that sound is 50% of content quality, especially in VR. Moreover, intuitive interactions that at least resemble those of the real world are critical.

High Fidelity is especially important for use cases where realism is required, such as simulations or product customization.

Functionality

Functionality focuses on what and how the user should do things in a virtual environment. As opposed to engagement and high fidelity, this group of features doesn't have to bring joy to the user nor look or be realistic – instead, they determine how much more efficient the user is in achieving a given task in VR, compared to using other mediums, such as desktop PC.

The third focus of VR, content, has been mostly ignored up to this point in "Post-Oculus" hype. That may be due to the fact that functionality was at the center of VR applications for over two decades, when technologies like CAVEs or powerwalls were in use. Up until the Oculus kickstarter in 2013, VR was used almost exclusively in high cost industries, such as automobile, as a way to reduce costs of prototyping. The trick was to exchange a physical prototype with a virtual one, but still be able to visualize it in real world scale and be able to put yourself in it, for example sit in the car prototype, or try to reach with your hand to a certain part inside a construction.

Using modern VR, high quality HMDs, intuitive interactions, far more compact hardware and reduced development costs mean limitations can be dissolved that stopped amazing industrial and functional improvements from being widely implemented and used.

Why would functional content be the heart of VR?

"Virtual Reality is a new medium", many VR enthusiasts say. But a new medium for what? A new way to play games or have fun? Isn't there more to it? Functional use cases are at the heart of other widely spread technologies. Yes, people use computers for gaming, but the vast majority use them for all kinds of private and professional work – from simple web searching to ... well... game development. Therefore, the vast majority of households in developed countries has now at least one unit, if not many. After computers came smartphones and tablets. And just as with computers, people do play games and watch movies on them, but mostly because they already have them, due to their professional purposes, such as mobile office (calendar, mail, document viewers and editors)..

Whenever I talk to a non-VR-enthusiast, such as my brother, they are not at all excited about it, because they simply do not see their own need for it. So, why someone who is neither a gamer nor is fascinated by this new medium as a "new way of storytelling" would spend more than $500 on goggles and another $1000 on a good enough PC, the specification of which is in excess of anything he would normally need?

The first question we need to ask ourselves is what unique possibilities does VR offer? Following in the footsteps of the great visionaries of VR in XXI century, such as Mike Alger, by using unlimited and 3D space of virtual worlds, we can finally leave rectangular 2D thinking and perception that standard displays forced us into. Nowadays we perceive and imagine digital content in form of rectangular, flat windows, the only way we access digital content is through 2D, rectangular screens – desktop, tablets, smartphones. Since virtual reality is not limited to a 2D screen, but through goggles is all around us, there is no technical reason why content should be limited by old rules. The possibilities are still hard to comprehend. As of now, many companies do attempt to create virtual workspace, e.g. Envelope VR or Virtual Desktop, but they are only making the first steps, by providing an increased display space – either increasing and stretching the screen around the user, or providing more virtual 2D screens.

Meanwhile, data visualization also uses the same advantage of unlimited 3D virtual space. A company called <u>SALT AND PEPPER Software Solutions</u>, took an interesting initiative in exploring a visualization of descriptive information. Over the last 3 years, since the new wave of VR began, there were a lot of attempts to visualize a VR ecosystem, e.g. by GreenlightVR or EUVR. Nevertheless, all those logos and categories were represented on a 2D plane. SALT AND PEPPER tapped into the power of VR and not only visualized information in 3D space, but also provided interaction that made the data easier to understand. All in all, it shows that through VR we can now not only visualize data that are neither quantitative nor qualitative (which technically was possible before, e.g. company organization graphs), but more importantly added an agency and interaction to data exploration, showing the use of VR to facilitate the comprehension of complex descriptive information.

Summary

If all that the virtual reality content market has to offer is entertainment, then the actual target group – people who want it and also can afford it - is rather small. However, if a VR ecosystem could provide something that people actually need, then the price would become a much smaller obstacle, and the target group would be far larger.

DEPLOYING VR INTO THE PUBLIC SPACE
by Kevin Williams

The Digital Out-of-Home Entertainment (DOE) sector is an emerging new landscape driven by a new and sophisticated audience visiting the plethora of out-of-home entertainment and leisure venues. These 'Digital Natives' are driven by a level of expected engagement fed by the connectivity and digital entertainment they have become accustomed to in their homes. Immersive Entertainment is the new platform of choice to satisfy this demand for experience out of home - and with new mixed reality technology - lessons learned in the previous explosion in interest in virtual reality (in the late Nineties) are being expounded on once again. With the use of VR playing a part in marketing and promotion, theme park attraction and amusement, the leisure and fitness (exer-gaming) industries, and even in edutainment applications in the out-of-home sphere, DOE looking to offer a wide variety of unique VR experiences to a mainstream audience that expensive consumer VR cannot yet achieve.

Figure 20: Treadmills, VR headsets and tracked devices are getting common in VR installations

It is important before we look too closely at the impact and role that VR (in the form of immersive entertainment) has played in the DOE sector, that we define this sector. The Out-of-Home Entertainment sector comprises the familiar theme park and amusement venue business (sometimes defined as pay-to-play), but also comprises the evolving landscapes for entertainment technology in hospitality, retail-tainment, edutainment and exer-gaming (as well as deployments in marketing and promotion). Here the 'Digital Native' guest to the public-space entertainment environment demands a level of entertainment and engagement that is equal, if not surpassing, what they have come to expect from their home entertainment and smart phone platforms.

Moving from the traditional screen based immersive approach, the deployment of totally immersive entertainment systems in this space are a result of a migration of technology from the military and training simulation sector being deployed in the large-scale entertainment environment. Following a number of tentative experiments – many of them led by leading theme park developers - the application of a field-able VR entertainment approach was achieved in the video amusement scene, with a number of platforms that built on the popularity of video amusement hardware in specialist venues, and used the latest (cumbersome) VR Head-Mounted Displays (HMD).

Even with thousands of these systems fielded, their limitations became all to obvious: reliability, resilience and effective and compelling content all proved to be issues. That and the high expense of hardware saw the sector implode and interest in consumer VR extinguished.

Jump forward to 2011 and a number of companies started to once again look at the opportunity that a totally encompassing and immersive environment could offer. Now powered by the latest CGi graphics, and fielded by a growing requirement for 'agency' and a game narrative from the modern attraction and amusement product. With the sophistication of the audience at a level where traditional passive ride experiences proved wanting, VR was given a second chance, partly also fuelled by the advances in mobile phone technology that offered screen and motion tracking technology that could offer a much more compelling approach.

The public-space sector also included one other element to ensure it offered a perfect medium for the evolution of VR into this sector. Unlike the restraints of consumer application, the DOE sector is prepared to pay much higher amounts to create an experience 'unachievable@home'! Where consumer VR is constantly mindful of the need to attract the mainstream, and the ballpark pricing needed to establish this level of adoption – the DOE sector is an enclosed organism that feeds itself, and is not restricted by such limitations. Long before the popularity of the crowd sourced VR HMD's, the DOE sector, especially in the marketing and promotional industries, was deploying VR, testing the waters and reviewing the successes and the issues.

At this point, there have been hundreds of marketing and promotional public-space enclosures, developed by leading marketing studios. Many have used early development kit HMD's to offer a compelling experience to promote a particular service or product. But with these developments, a knowledge of what works and what does not in the deployment of VR in the Out-of-Home environment has been added to the collected information from the previous (phase three) approach to VR in the 90's. We now see with this phase four of VR adoption, key approaches towards utilising the technology within the DOE environment.

The first is Attractions, the theme park industry familiar of using the latest technology to enthral their audience. Within the application of VR in this sector we have seen two current popular approaches – the first being the use of the technology as an additional component to an existing ride: a number of rollercoaster and flat-rides in operation have been 're-booted' with the use of HMD's syntonizer to the motion of the ride vehicle, while representing a virtual experience to riders on mobile VR HMD's. The other approach is the development of totally new attractions that incorporate VR technology directly into the creation of new platforms. The ability to create a totally repurposable attraction offering great benefits for operators constantly looking for the next thrill for a highly demanding audience.

The second approach to VR in DOE is the Stand-Alone Game System. The creation of game platforms that can be deployed in a wide variety of venues looking to offer an entertainment mix has seen a number of companies create motion seat and motion capsule platforms that incorporate a VR display element. Lessons learned from 4D and 5D theatre development as deployed into a VR stand-alone platform enabled the chance of constant renewal via new software when the previous titles start to flag.

The third approach to VR in public-space is Location-Based Entertainment (LBE), also described by some as 'Arena-Scale' VR. As learned from operating lasertag style facilities, the ability to encourage a repeat visitation to a unique franchise venue offering a totally compelling immersive experience is an obvious one. The high price unveiled by the current developers of consumer VR (for both their hardware, the PC to run it, and the content demands) has seen much of the original anticipation in home VR start to wane, but in offering a stand-alone experience in a simple to deploy 'box' to local areas, the opportunity to use the latest wireless backpack VR delivery systems, in multi-player enclosures – even employing theatrical effects - has enthused a growing industry of new developers, with even film production companies excited by this offering as a component to address flagging cinema business. The LBE approach to VR is seen by many as a means to a rebirth in the popularity of arcade gaming and registration of the highly social opportunity this brings to the VR experience, as against the individual VR consumer's generally solitary experience.

The fourth of the current approaches is that offered by LAN Gaming or Internet Center application – seen before in the PC gaming scene where expensive PC workstations were monetized when deployed in clusters in specialist retail facilities – with players able to compete in online-gaming tournaments, using hardware they were unable to afford or install in their homes. This is also true of the millions that use the Internet via retail based terminals, again amortizing the price of hardware and required connections. As seen with LAN gaming, a number of corporations are looking towards adding VR to the mix of services they offer, even hoping that LAN based facilities could become the showrooms for the VR opportunity, and build a groundswell of support.

However, there needs to be a word of caution in the consideration of deploying consumer hardware and software into public-space application. A number of would-be operators have come unstuck when trying to use consumer hardware in DOE environments; all consumer electronics and content are covered under warranty and terns of usage – the majority of which prohibit the use of the products in commercial application, and restrict usage and sale. This is not a total prohibition of consumer VR in LAN and Internet facility use, as already a number of agreements between operators and manufacturers have started to be made, allowing specialist deployment of their systems in selected venues, needing to ensure that the platforms offer the best approach for the unique needs of the venue.

These are by no means the only possible approaches, and feverish activity is being carried out behind closed doors at numerous research and development operations linked to content and facility operations; leading corporations in these respective fields have moved off the fence to start to invest in R&D in this field, and a steady number of high profile announcements seem to punctuate the media regarding a DOE approach to VR.

Finally, the lessons learned from the DOE's investment in VR application offers a salient lesson for those hoping to jump blindly into the VR scene. The most important area of consideration are the requirements of utilising HMD's in the public-space. As with 3D glasses, the entertainment sector has created a detailed approach to hygiene in this environment. For VR HMD's the mantra of following the three-R's has become law – the need to be mindful of 'Reliability', offering a system that can be easily cleaned and serviced, and works for all percentiles. The need for 'Resilience', where the HMD is not a medium for foreign objects or the transference of bacteria. But also it has to be 'Robust', able to be dropped, knocked, and man handled by scores of users, and still give great service.

Along with the three-R's, there are also the lessons learned regarding the best way to immerse the user within a virtual experience, the rules needed to be obeyed in offering the best experience to the widest audience and avoiding the dangers and pitfalls associated with the issues of 'Sim-Sickness'. Issues only now being considered by the consumer games sector include the unique user experience of the DOE market, with game experiences lasting minutes rather than hoped-for hours, opening brand new knowledge towards what can and cannot be achieved by this amazing and compelling technology.

VR ANALYTICS INTERVIEW WITH KEVIN WILLIAMS

Questions by Chuck Ian Gordon

Figure 21: Kevin Williams (left) and Chuck Ian Gordon (right)
on a VR panel at the University of Murcia, Spain in September 2015

Q1: With VR/AR Analytics it is possible to track the consumers viewing experience: where does he/she look at for how long, does he/she track objects or people? We can combine this - where technically possible - with position information in roomscale VR or even eventspace VR (thinking about installations like the void). We also can add information about the pose and movements of people (skeleton projection into real bodies). With the advent of eye tracking technologies (like the vive) or facial expression analysis (www.affectiva.com) and body function tracking from smart watches we will be able to look even deeper into people's minds. What data collection opportunities can be expected for DOE VR installations?

KWP: The theme park industry has been tracking statistically data of guest experiences since the days of the first ticketing systems. With the latest OOH based technology we have been looking at the utilization of the venue and the placement of attractions and services, but also at the dwell time and progression through the venues and how this can be maximized. In particular based on the development of a return visit revenue stream, the need to create an entertainment environment that offers a compelling experience is essential. The use of interactive narrative and game elements

76

to the attractions is another factor where before-during-after park visiting data will need to be collected, linked to the social media / social experience data supporting web and app services. Much of what has been seen in the OOH digital signage sector is being applied in the park and entertainment venue business, already some developers looking at monitoring the guest's level of engagement in the entertainment towards shaping the interactive narrative as just one example.

Q2: Thinking about AR the room scale could be even enhanced to the world (combining e.g. google maps' history of my location with consumed AR contents and my reactions there - like http://www.cluetivity.com/ : What AR Analytics developments and combinations with VR / AR DOE can you imagine?

KWP: What we call 'mixed reality' for the combining of AR and VR as well as other digital mediums such as 3D projection mapping and touchscreen systems - the mixing of this will first be seen in new versions of the Lasertag environment, already experimented with in the sector, the use of a targeting tracker that the player could wear while traversing the lasertag arena presents a serious opportunity to expand the gaming experience and build on the players evolving skill levels. As with much in this sector, the use of already proven military and training technology is then turned to entertainment application - wearable systems have already been used by military and you can expect to see versions of these deployed in entertainment.

KWP: Regarding other Mixed Reality deployments, the biggest move will be in the guest information and ticketing approach- the use of wearables in the entertainment environment has proven a compelling opportunity, as seen with Disney's deployment of MagicBand. How much of the future of this approach will be in the data, than with the physical item it reports too needs to be seen, but the benefits of supplying guest information, tracking their progress and allowing them access to payment and keycard services via their personalized device is a approach to technology far beyond seen in current consumer application.

Q3: Besides the improvement of the VR experience itself - which is a very important goal - who do you think is interested in the data that can be collected and for what purpose (e.g. creating marketing profiles of people, determining preferences)?

KWP: The usage of the collected data falls into three areas:
- back-of-house: Meaning the facility operation, along with improving the

ride experience; marketing and promotional teams are keen to use the data to help shape their presentation and chart the level of investment to support the required attendance to the venue. This also helps in charting the life-span of attractions and experiences, and even in considering the addition of a new gate to the venue. Also in these changing times the need to track guests for security reasons grows, and the use of smart data collection to check unusual behaviour or dangerous intent are elements of all venues' future warning systems.

- front-of-house: Meaning the guest and services operation, the ability for the guest to track members of their party, track their popular attractions and favoured routes and services, or even just know where they parked their car - the ability to offer this data to the guests is essential to maximise their experience and build a rapport with the guest. For guest services the ability to know if a guest is allergic to a food item, has health needs, or is just in difficulty, can assist with the security and safety of the park, the ability also to offer specialized services to VIP and group visitors is a new revenue stream that needs to be considered, as seen in the hospitality sector.

- Sponsors: This group represent companies and corporations advertising within the park or promoting their brand through sponsorship of development and attractions. To see that they are receiving value for their investment access to data such as guest satisfaction within the park, and guest engagement with the experience need to be presented. This can also include the need for this information to be presented along with the revenue figures to shareholders and investors.

Q4: What critical aspects do you see in collecting personal behavioural data and adding it to personal profiles regarding data privacy (the consumer's viewpoint) and how do you think could companies providing VR/AR DOE proactively deal with those concerns?

KWP: As seen with Walt Disney using 'hand-scan' rather than finger print technology for the validation of their VIP and Guest pass systems, the need to be mindful of data security and possible law enforcement requests for access to data retained on guests' visits is an issue. The illegal use of park tickets as psuedo-money to pay for illicit items is a case in point, as is the Dave & Busters data breach that saw credit card details stolen. Separating the data from the actual details of the guests' account, and the retention of the data in a secure manner are all issues. But also as stated above, the use of data to evaluate guests intent on property and to block criminal behaviour is an issue, which is also linked to increased anti-terrorist procedure deployed by some parks.

All entertainment venues that collect data will need to have a level of security regarding retained information, and also need to be able to utilize the information in emergencies. The entertainment venue of the future may use existing smart techniques to direct guests off property, and also for zoning areas off, staggering evacuation and so avoiding bottlenecks. Smart information on the number and type of guest in certain areas, data collected from their smart ticketing or tracking tech, means that parks will be able to manage their safety requirements at a higher level, so saving lives and minimizing injuries.

Towards the farming of data - and offering this to corporations outside of the entertainment operation - for the time being it is best to keep this information internal and to help grow the operator's brand and properties. In order to ensure guest loyalty to the brand, the knowledge that the information is retained only to be used by the park, and that the data is not specific to their personal details is essential. It would seem only as linked to games and rewards will this data ever be seen as usable, and even then the degree of circulation of score, preference and general interests will all have to be monitored to ensure guest respect and compliance with its use.

Q5: Thank you for those interesting insights, Kevin!

2016 VIRTUAL REALITY ANALYTICS WEB SUMMIT, SAN FRANCISCO

Produced by March 15-16, 2016
Excerpts from the Executive Report
With friendly permission of Clifton Dawson,
Founder & President, GreenlightVR
www.greenlightvr.com
Selection of information subset by Joerg Osarek

Figure 22: What better place to hold a summit about Virtual Reality Analytics –
close to the Golden Gate Bridge in San Francisco

Prelude: Some Personal Words

I had the honour to moderate the panel "Going Deep: Mining Experiential and Behavioral Data in VR" with Sunny Webb, Senior R&D Principal and Accenture and Geoff Skowe, CEO of Fishbowl VR. The panelists, speakers, attendees and numerous topics of the complete event made some points clear to me.

- Virtual Reality Analytics and later AR Analytics are serious topics meant to stay and to enrich our business intelligence world.

- The development yet is barely noticed throughout Europe, especially in Germany. Major players in Northern America, especially the US are already far more advanced on their way to building our new VR analytics platforms.

- The task given to us all is now to learn how to build and manage this new extension to classic business intelligence.

Event Overview

The 2016 Virtual Reality Analytics Web Summit took place on March 16th. With over 200 people attending either the Web Summit or the Welcome Reception on March 15th, the 2016 Virtual Reality Analytics Web Summit brought together industry experts to discuss analytics, big data, and hottopics for the VR/AR industry.

Over the course of two days, attendees heard from 25 speakers as they shared their thoughts and answered questions during seven keynote sessions, and a vendor showcase. Each 50minute sessions offered a look into the virtual reality industry, and the emergence of the analytics and best practices for the industry.

More details can be found in Greenlight VR's 2016 Industry Report (released mid April 2016).

There is also a video recording of the event and the complete executive summary available at

http://www.greenlightvr.com/events/2016-analytics-web-summit.

March 15th: Welcome Reception, Keynote Speaker: Jesse Schell, Schell Games

The 2016 Virtual Reality Analytics Web Summit kicked off with a networking and cocktail reception and the Mechanics' Institute in Downtown San Francisco. The evening featured keynote speaker Jesse Schell, CEO of Schell Games and Distinguished Professor of the Practice of Entertainment Technology at Carnegie Mellon University (CMU) Entertainment Technology Center (ETC). Schell unveiled his latest "Predictions of VR/AR through 2025" . Predictions ranged from the impact that visual storytelling will have to looking ahead to the "2017 CES show, where there will be at least fifty different headsets on display," according to Schell's presentation. The general agreement among those in attendance was that major progress has been made in the industry, and Jesse Schell's predictions embodied those discussions that took place among nearly 75 people in attendance.

Some of the 40 predictions Jesse Schell made (which I leave uncommented) were:

- 1. VR is finally here, It isn't a fad any longer. VR headsets will permanently be in the consumer market.

- 2. 8 million Gamer VR headsets will be sold in 2016. This estimate excludes mobile VR headsets like the Samsung Gear VR.

- 3. 4 mobile headsets will ship for each gamer headset.

- 4. VR headset shipments will double every year.

- 26. In 2017, every US State Fair will have a VR Attraction.

- 27. By 2020 there will be at least 20 VR coasters worldwide. Schell said he beat his prediction – when he first made this prediction last year there were four VR roller coaster rides like this. Now there are 24.

- 28. By 2025 location based VR events analogous to the bowling alley with AR Glasses will be a thing.

- 31. By 2025, AR experiences synced with TV will be a thing.

- 32. At all levels in education augmented reality lectures will be popular by 2025. The teacher and students strap on VR goggles and all go to the same microscopic or telescopic place together.

- 34. By 2018, gamers will wear narrow glasses or get contacts that fit into VR headgear.

- 35. By 2020, really hardcore gamers will have headsets fitted with prescription lenses.

- 36. By 2018 eye tracking VR headsets will be available and bringing eye to eye contact into games and apps responsive to eye movement.

- 37. By 2020 foveated rendering will exist. This type of rendering increases resolution at specific focus points – for example where the eye is focuses.

- 39. When the difference between reality and virtual reality can't be discerned with vision and hearing virtual touch will be the next development.

- 40. Robots will touch us by 2025 to fulfill the need for touch to complement the senses of vision and hearing.

The following sections list extracs of the summary of the different panels.

New Horizons in VR Intelligence and Analytics

Virtual reality will open a new opportunity for interaction with information across many fields. Companies can utilize virtual reality as a way to better communicate firsthand information on the job.

This could allow global companies to collaborate over a project more efficiently than a video conference currently affords. This expansion on companies' ability to communicate has measurable improvements to business productivity. Businesses can use virtual reality to bring together big data and analytics in real time to show projections and analyzations. This can save time, money and assets.

Enhancing VR Game Experiences with Leading-Edge Analytics

Leading analytics software has helped better understand what gamers like in virtual reality game play. Virtual reality and the gaming industry is uncharted waters as companies are still experimenting to learn how to best proceed with creation of games.

The panelists report that matching mechanics to controls in the game are the most comfortable for players as measured in their studies. Gamers have a better response when they are able to do the action they are performing in the game. The sense of immersion felt in their experiments adds to the player's focus on game play and causes players to block out the outside world.

"There are many reasons to use a virtual reality environment for data," said Karl Maddix from Masters of Pie. "360 space, immersion and body and hand tracking, taken together, can allow for a better interaction with data than just on a desktop. Essentially, VR has way more possibilities to provide data beyond what many people do with desktop analytics"

Going Deep: Mining Experiential and Behavioral Data in VR

According to Sunny Webb, Senior R&D Principal at Accenture Technology Labs, the AR/VR market will reach $148 billion by 2020. Webb detailed the immersive technology spectrum (i.e. replacement, augmented, single channel, spatially aware) and shared results from recent Accenture studies. During the session, Webb shared highlights from client studies. She noted that as clients increase immersiveness in digital experiences, users rank higher amounts of:

- Engagement: 18% more engaged

- Influence: 16% more influence

- Retaining knowledge: 4% more natural & 15% increased sufficiency

Fishbowl VR offers on demand VR app testing services that let you outsource your VR app testing processes completely. This is another example that cloud computing and Xaas (everything as a service) also will be part of of modern VR and VR analytics architectures.

Leveraging integrated VR Advertising and Analytics Platforms

Advertising will need to be more immersive and interactive in order to be effective in virtual reality. The panel was unanimous in their belief that the creative behind VR advertising experiences is key to a successful ROI.

"The impulse in moving from video will be to apply it to VR," said Framestore VR's Tyler Hopf. "But applying preroll to VR won't work. People won't want to be placed inside [an ad]. So we have to figure out ways to create valuable ad experiences."

"VR is the most data rich medium out there," said EEVO CEO Alejandro Dinsmore. "A key to creating compelling experiences is to listen to the analytics to make the experience better. In VR, we have positional head tracking data, which means we can Overlay 3d objects on top of video, such as dynamic product placement. We can place dynamic 3d objects in blank spaces and measure the feedback."

This brings up another "native" aspect of VR beyond creation of ad experiences: new analytics. There too, it will take native thinking and not imposing old metrics on new formats and media consumption patterns.

Harnessing Big Data for Live Sports in VR

With Virtually Live recently announcing a new partnership with STATS LLC, the discussion focused on how the company use sports data to recreate live game experiences in VR using Big Data and allowing multiple viewpoints as the whole scene is recreated. However, Impallomeni estimated that putting you right in the stadium is still 5-10 years off.

Illuminating VR User Engagement via High-End Cameras

Traditional Hollywood films took 30-40 years of experimentation before understanding how to properly film. "Analytics can accelerate that process" for virtual reality," said Andrew Walkingshaw, Head of Data Engineering at Jaunt VR. Analytics can help figuring out instead of guessing what people want to watch. This can translate into getting people to pay attention to what you want them to pay attention to rather than hoping they will pay attention to it.

Plumbing Audience Insight in New VR Retailing Environments

Virtual reality can affect consumer buying trends because buying patterns have been changing in recent years. There might be a new megatrend in including virtual reality in the retail process. VR Showrooms – for example – from Audi indicate that the known retail key performance indicators change significantly when you include a VR showroom. The rate of sales is increased, you need way fewer cars and 50% of people who visited the VR showroom and bought a car didn't take a test drive.

Virtual Reality Analytics Showcase

Alexander Haque from Retinad VR demonstrated their VR heatmaps similar to heatmaps known from retail store shopping analytics.

About Greenlight VR

Greenlight VR is the industry leader in business intelligence for the virtual reality global market. By maintaining the most comprehensive dataset of information on companies and consumer behavior for virtual reality, Greenlight VR provides global technology companies, Fortune 500 brands, and innovative startups proprietary research and advice to make better strategic decisions. Greenlight VR also publishes the annual Virtual Reality Industry Report, purchased by hundreds of companies worldwide. For more information visit their website: www.greenlightvr.com

This page is reserved for your Virtual Reality Notes...

This page is reserved for your Augmented Reality Notes…

This page is reserved for your Real Reality Notes…